NAVIGATING NONFICTION

by Alice Boynton and Wiley Blevins

ISBN-13 978-0-439-78294-4
ISBN-10 0-439-78294-5

1 2 3 4 5 6 7 8 9 10   66   15 14 13 12 11 10 09 08 07

TABLE OF CONTENTS

TABLE OF CONTENTS

FOREWORD

Today's teachers know far more about reading instruction than at any time in the past. In the classrooms that I visit, teachers effectively engage students in reading experiences that help students understand that reading is an active, meaning making process that requires critical comprehension skills like inferring, predicting, summarizing, and evaluating. Students regularly learn to apply a wide range of comprehension strategies to narrative texts including folktales, plays, realistic fiction, historical fiction, and poetry.

Within the past few years, however, the attention of the professional community has turned to the reading of nonfiction type texts. State standards now require that students at every grade level be taught to read the expository text found in newspapers, magazines, information trade books, or the Internet. Why is it crucial that students learn to read this type of text? Quite simply, because their success in school and the workplace depends on it. By sixth grade, 80 percent of school reading tasks involve informational text. Furthermore, standardized tests, which generally assess the ability to read content-related passages in a variety of areas, are predominantly expository. In addition, most of the reading required by the Internet involves expository text.

> "By sixth grade, 80 percent of school reading tasks involve informational text."

The skills students need to negotiate nonfiction texts are different from those needed to comprehend narrative text, and teaching these skills presents new challenges to teachers. Comments from the teachers in my classes illustrate this point: "I never even knew informational texts were mentioned in the standards until we talked about it in class." "I teach stories; I don't know what to do with nonfiction texts." "I never thought about the differences between fiction and nonfiction before."

Navigating Nonfiction: Tools for Reading Success in the Content Areas provides a teacher-friendly toolkit of strategies that can help teachers support their students as they face the challenges associated with nonfiction texts. The lessons in the student worktexts demonstrate how to read nonfiction text features like headings, maps, charts, and time lines and provide opportunities for application of student learning through the reading of authentic, engaging

> "Navigating Nonfiction... a valuable resource for preparing today's students for the reading demands of the twenty-first century."

science and social studies passages. These carefully scaffolded lessons also focus on the five most commonly found expository text structures. In addition, graphic organizers and writing frames engage students in reading and writing about the texts. Research clearly indicates the value of such activities in developing comprehension.

The teacher's guide provides easy-to-use lessons for teaching students how to navigate text and deal with the challenges posed by nonfiction text features and structures. It also includes solid suggestions for engaging students in meaningful before, during, and after reading activities that promote the critical-thinking skills necessary for success with nonfiction texts.

The *Navigating Nonfiction* series will not only provide students with practice in reading expository text, but, in the hands of an effective teacher, it will help students think deeply about how to approach this text type in a variety of forms. Teachers are sure to find the *Navigating Nonfiction* series a valuable resource for preparing today's students for the reading demands of the twenty-first century.

—Barbara Moss

PROGRAM COMPONENTS

Navigating Nonfiction provides a complete nonfiction reading worktext program. It is designed to target those skills students need to tackle the nonfiction text they will encounter in content area textbooks and in the reading curriculum. In the program, you will find the following components.

Student WorkText

- Contains 30 weeks of instruction: 10 scaffolded instructional units of 3 weeks each
- Focuses on nonfiction text features and text structures
- Provides step-by-step strategies for navigating nonfiction

- Follows simple 3-step unit organization. Step 1: text feature taught in isolation. Step 2: text feature practiced in context. Step 3: text structure taught in context; text feature included
- Correlates to grade-level social studies and science standards
- Contains high-interest articles

Teacher's Guide

- Targets critical nonfiction reading skills essential for academic reading success
- Contains simple, easy-to-follow instructional routines
- Provides explicit teaching models and *Think Alouds*

Text Structures Poster

- Visual snapshot of the five nonfiction structures
- Great classroom reference

WHAT'S INSIDE THE TEACHER'S GUIDE?

FOCUS ON TEXT FEATURES
Weeks 1 and 2 of each unit

- Teach/Practice/Apply lesson organization

- Everything you need to know about the text feature

- Focuses on key points to model. Great for novice teachers

- Grade specific, standards aligned

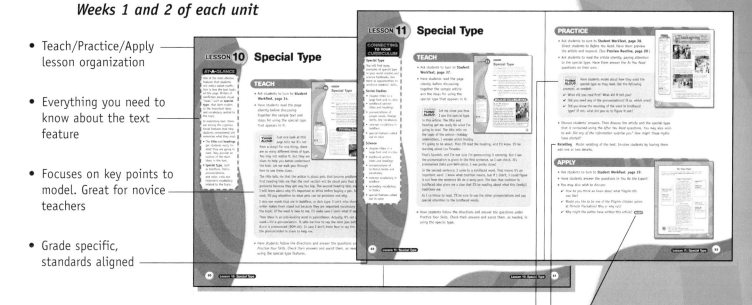

- Accelerates internalization of skills and strategies
- Builds and demonstrates comprehension
- NAEP connection

FOCUS ON TEXT STRUCTURE
Week 3 of each unit

- Predictable lesson organization

- Informal assessment

- Key concept words in context

- Independent application of skills

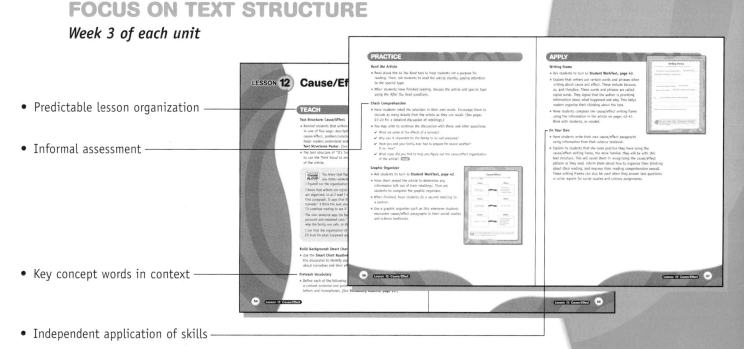

WHAT'S INSIDE THE STUDENT WORKTEXT?

FOCUS ON TEXT FEATURES
Weeks 1 and 2 of each unit

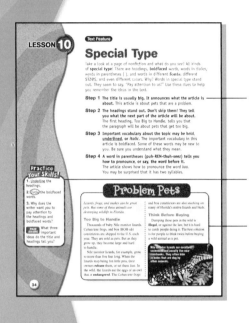

- Step-by-step tools for understanding and using text feature

- Interactive guided practice

- Example of text feature

- Text feature in context; alternates science and social studies content

- Interactive guided practice

- Discussion prompt, with pair-share response

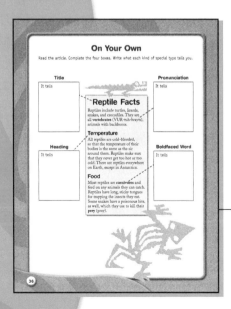

- Independent application

FOCUS ON TEXT STRUCTURE
Week 3 of each unit

- Before/During/After student roadmap

- Preteach vocabulary with graphic organizer

- Interactive guided practice

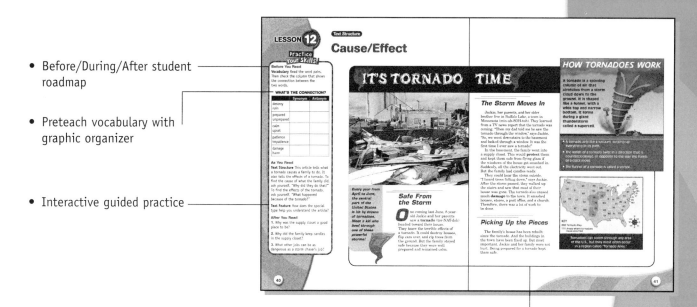

- Curriculum-connected authentic text that includes text feature

- Linked to text structure of article to serve as basis for retelling

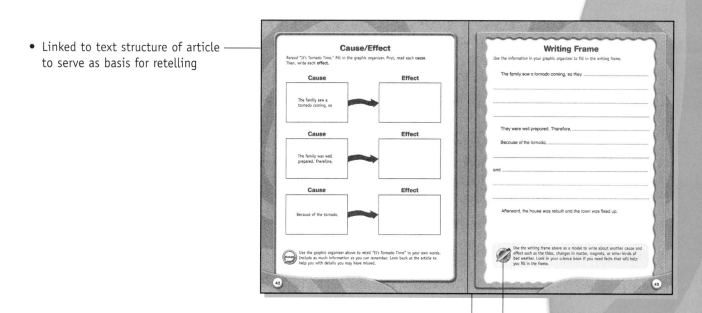

- Connects text structure to writing to help students internalize structures

- Writing application connected to curriculum

WHAT IS NONFICTION?

This may seem like an easy question. But, what *really* is nonfiction? Nonfiction, also called expository text, provides information. Its purpose is to explain, inform, or persuade. You may be surprised by how much nonfiction surrounds us every day—newspapers, subway maps, instructions for changing a vacuum-cleaner bag, recipes, and the dreaded VCR manual. Teaching students to read nonfiction, therefore, is essential as we teach them to develop as readers.

In Grades 4 through 6, the emphasis in reading instruction changes from learning to read to reading to learn (Chall, 1983). As students progress through the grades, more and more of their reading is done in nonfiction, or expository, materials—content area textbooks, reference books, periodicals, and informative articles on the Internet, for example. The main purpose for reading these texts is to acquire information. Students need explicit instruction on how to approach these texts; it's a mistake to assume that if students can read a chapter book they can automatically read and understand a textbook.

Unlike a narrative, which tells a story, expository text explains facts and concepts, many of them complex and difficult to understand. These texts use a whole different set of features and structures, which pose many challenges to students if not explained and discussed. In addition, some students may still struggle with basic reading skills, making the challenge of nonfiction even more daunting. Ignoring the needs of students leaves them further behind; we need to offer them additional instruction and practice with reading skills and strategies.

WHY IS NONFICTION CHALLENGING?

Content

Reading and understanding expository text requires a high level of abstract thinking. Readers are called on not only to comprehend ideas that may be difficult but also to extrapolate and remember the significant main ideas and to integrate them with other information from prior knowledge. Students must be able to recognize complex causes and effects, compare and contrast ideas, synthesize information from a variety of sources, and evaluate proposed solutions to problems as they read. This is tough work for developing readers!

Vocabulary

Another major difference between narrative and expository text is the vocabulary that readers encounter. Each content area has its own specialized terms that children are not exposed to in stories—or in conversation either. Many of these terms are polysyllabic words that are more difficult to decode and pronounce. Here are some examples from Grade 3 science and social studies textbooks: *photosynthesis, paleontologist, nonprofit, transcontinental, erosion*. To compound the difficulty, many of the terms have unfamiliar meanings, such as Earth's *crust*.

Text Features

Added to the demands of content and vocabulary are the special features of expository text—how expository text physically looks on the page. Unlike narrative text, which moves along from one chapter to the next without interruption other than an occasional chapter title or an illustration, expository text is frequently interrupted by headings and subheadings, pronunciations in parentheses, labels, footnotes, and a variety of graphics that must be carefully examined. Consider a typical nonfiction page.

A student faced with a page of expository text may be so overwhelmed by the physical presentation of the material that he or she doesn't know where to begin!

Text Structures

Another challenge to readers is the organizational structure of expository text. In contrast to narrative text, in which the plot flows from one event to the next, expository materials usually segment a topic into various subtopics. The content is commonly structured in one of the following ways:

1. cause/effect,
2. compare/contrast,
3. problem/solution,
4. sequence or time order,
5. listing or description, or
6. a combination of the above.

In each new piece of expository text, readers must uncover the organizational pattern in order to comprehend the relationship of ideas. Research has shown a strong link between students' comprehension of expository text and their understanding
of the way the text is organized [Seidenberg's study; Pearson & Fielding's study; and Weaver & Kintsch's study (as cited in Carnine, Silbert, & Kameenui, 1997)].

Even if all these challenges make our heads swim, we must not forget the tremendous payoff that teaching our students to read nonfiction will have.

Most children acquire the knowledge of narrative structures naturally, through years of hearing, reading, and telling narrative stories.

WHY IS NONFICTION IMPORTANT?

The ability to understand and write nonfiction is essential for school achievement [Seidenberg's study (as cited in Carnine et al., 1997)]. Students will encounter a larger number of nonfiction texts as they progress through the grades, each posing special challenges.

Nonfiction Text and Standardized Tests: The Connection

With the passage of the No Child Left Behind Act in 2002, students must take high-stakes, end-of-year tests to determine whether they can be promoted. These tests ask students to read both fiction and nonfiction, compare the two texts, and respond to them in writing. Teaching students to navigate and comprehend nonfiction texts throughout the year is far preferable to the sudden and intense test-prep practice in the weeks leading to the test.

Increased World Knowledge

Teaching students to navigate and read nonfiction texts gives them access to a large body of important and useful information—information that they are not exposed to in everyday conversations but need in order to succeed in school, develop lifelong learning habits, pursue their interests, gain necessary skills, and become well-informed and responsible citizens. Plus, learning about the world around us is fascinating!

HOW CAN WE PREPARE STUDENTS?

Research shows that understanding how text is organized helps readers construct meaning [Dickson, Simmons, & Kameenui's study (as cited in CORE, 1999)]. It follows that students need explicit instruction in text presentation and text structure as an aid to comprehending expository text. If students learn to read the signposts that are guides to the organization of a particular piece of nonfiction, they will be better equipped to navigate their way through the material.

One approach to teaching students how to read nonfiction—such as content area textbooks—is to build students' skills in identifying and using the various tools that are characteristic of this type of text. That is, we focus on teaching students how to navigate nonfiction text. For example:

- Learning to **preview** the title, headings, and subheadings in a chapter of social studies or science text will enable students to anticipate the main ideas that will be covered.

- Knowing how to use **text features**—special type and graphic aids, such as diagrams, charts, graphs, and time lines—will allow readers to take additional meaning from them rather than viewing them as a disruption to the flow of the text. In addition, it will help students integrate this information with that provided by the text.

- Identifying the **text structure** will promote students' understanding and retention. Is the author comparing and contrasting life on the frontier with life in the cities? Is the text describing the physical characteristics of dinosaurs?

Nonfiction surrounds us. The reasons for teaching our students efficient and effective strategies for tackling this type of text are compelling. What we must ask ourselves now is *How?*

LET'S NAVIGATE!

LEARNING ABOUT TEXT FEATURES

Let's take a closer look at the organization of a typical nonfiction lesson in this program. It focuses students' attention on how to navigate the text and how to identify and use "tools," such as headings and boldfaced words, that serve as aids to comprehension. In addition, many students need advance preparation in how to read and interpret the graphic aids they are most likely to meet in nonfiction text—maps, charts, graphs, diagrams, and time lines. Therefore, the lesson also introduces one type of graphic aid at a time and teaches students how to read and interpret it. In subsequent lessons, the same feature will be embedded in authentic text just as students would encounter it in their science and social studies reading. At this stage, students will practice reading text, stopping to refer to a graphic, and then returning to the text.

Nonfiction Tools
- ✔ Diagrams
- ✔ Maps
- ✔ Charts
- ✔ Time Lines
- ✔ Special Type
- ✔ Primary Sources
- ✔ Graphs
- ✔ Online Features
- ✔ Multiple Features in Text

LEARNING ABOUT TEXT STRUCTURES

Now let's focus on a text structure lesson. Informational texts have both a content and a structure. The structure is the organizational pattern *within* the text. It ties the ideas together. Understanding the structure enables students to better comprehend the content. The first task is being able to identify the structure of a piece of text. The next task is knowing how to use that structure to organize the content [Just & Carpenter's study (as cited in Alvermann & Phelps, 1998)].

The Five Most Common Structures of Nonfiction

Just like fiction, which has plot structure that students must learn and recognize, nonfiction follows basic structures. Five kinds of text structures, or patterns of organization, are commonly found in informational texts.

1. **Description or listing** provides information, such as facts, characteristics, and attributes about a subject, event, person, or concept. This organization is the most common pattern found in textbooks. Here is an example:

   The dinosaurs were four to eight feet long, about the size of kangaroos. They had small heads and long necks, and they walked on two or four legs.

2. **Sequence or time order** presents a series of events that take place chronologically. The author traces the sequence or the steps in the process from start to finish. An example is:

   Trouble had been brewing for more than 10 years. In 1763 Britain defeated France in the French and Indian War. Britain then tried to tighten control over its 13 colonies and tax the colonies more heavily.

3. **Compare/contrast** points out the likenesses and/or differences between two or more subjects. For example:

   The cheetah can run 70 mph. In the 1996 Olympic games, Michael Johnson set a world record and captured the gold medal when he ran 200 meters in 19.32 seconds. That's 23 mph.

4. **Cause/effect** attempts to explain why something happens—how facts or events (causes) lead to other facts or events (effects). A single cause often has several effects. Also, a single event may have several causes. This paragraph describes causes and effects:

   As the left plate slides down into the earth, it enters the hot mantle. Rocks in the sliding plate begin to melt, and they form magma.

5. **Problem/solution** describes a problem and presents one or more solutions to that problem. The following is an example:

   Environmentalists are battling to save remaining native species. Scientists and private citizens are attempting to preserve 4,000 acres on the island of Hawaii by literally fencing them off against alien invader species.

Things would be nice and simple if every piece of expository text were neatly written in one clearly identifiable pattern. However, informational text is often complex, and an author may not use one text structure exclusively throughout a long piece of writing. It is more likely that only a section of the text will be organized in a single pattern. For example, a chapter about weather in a science textbook may:

- first discuss different kinds of weather conditions *(description/listing),*
- then go on to explain the patterns that result in particular kinds of weather *(cause/effect),*
- follow up with a discussion of when a snowstorm officially becomes a blizzard or when a rainstorm is classified as a hurricane *(compare/contrast),* and finally
- close with what to do in the event of severe weather, such as a tornado *(problem/solution).*

The goal of text structure is to enable students to recognize and use these structures flexibly so that they can make meaning from nonfiction texts.

Signal Words as Clues to Text Structures

A good writer connects ideas within the text with words and phrases. These *connectives,* or *ties,* can act as signals to an informed reader who is trying to identify the text structure. The chart below shows some of the connectives that authors use to signal different text structures and the message they transmit to readers.

TEXT STRUCTURE	SIGNAL WORDS AND PHRASES	SIGNAL TO READER
Description or list	to begin with for example for instance most important in front, beside, near	A list or set of characteristics will follow.
Sequence or time order	first, second, third before on (date) not long after after that next at the same time finally then following	A sequence of events or steps in a process is being described.
Compare/contrast	like, unlike but in contrast on the other hand however both also, too, as well as	Likenesses and differences are being presented and/or discussed.
Cause/effect or Problem/solution	therefore consequently so this led to as a result because if . . . then	Evidence of cause(s) and effect(s) will be given or problems and solutions will be described.

We can see why readers must be explicitly taught to recognize and use text structures. Text structures are critical for constructing meaning, yet they are difficult to identify for the developing reader. Therefore, in week three of each unit, two things happen:

1. **Students focus their attention on text structure.** They are taught what the text structures are and what clues they can use to identify the organization of a particular piece of writing. Students get multiple exposures to each of the text structures discussed above. And, of course, they will have many additional opportunities to apply what they have learned in their classroom content area reading. All of this practice will enable students to internalize the skill and become sufficiently proficient to use it independently.

2. **The reading selection also provides students with another opportunity to practice and apply the skills** they were previously taught. The features and graphic aids that were the focus of weeks one and two in the unit are embedded in a longer passage of informational text. A chart, for example, might be part of a science article just as students would encounter it in their content area reading. Students will practice integrating information from the chart with the information in the text.

INSTRUCTIONAL ROUTINES

BUILDING BACKGROUND

Let's stop for a moment to talk about how you can prepare students *before* they begin reading the content area selection.

Prior knowledge is the background knowledge of the subject matter that a reader brings to a text; in other words, what a person already knows about the topic based on that person's experiences and beliefs. Research (Cooper, 1993; Lapp, Flood, & Farnan, 1996) shows that activating prior knowledge before reading:

- helps you assess the accuracy of what students already know.
- helps you identify gaps in students' prior knowledge—information that students need to bring to the text in order to construct meaning.
- helps readers construct meaning by making a connection between the new information and what is already known.
- helps readers recall the new information after it is read.
- helps create motivation for learning.

Your role as a teacher is to provide instructional scaffolds. Like the use of scaffolds in construction, you support, or lift up, students so that they can achieve what they cannot achieve by themselves. As Vacca and Vacca (1999) state, "instructional scaffolding allows teachers to support readers' efforts to make sense of texts while showing them how to use strategies that will, over time, lead to independent reading." So, while you are not preteaching the information students will read, you are filling in instructional gaps or dealing with misconceptions that would otherwise impede learning as they read.

Smart Charts

How can you bridge the gap between what students know and what they need to know? One way is to use a Smart Chart (Scholastic RED, 2002). The difference between a Smart Chart and its classic cousin, the KWL chart, is the additional first column—Background. This column helps you bring students "up to speed" in terms of background information necessary to make meaning from the text. A Smart Chart:

- prompts students to think about what they already know.
- provides an efficient way for you to give students important background information that they need to know.
- encourages students to organize what they know, what they want to know, and what they learned from a reading selection.
- helps students set a purpose for reading.
- provides a place for students to review and record what they learned.

There are many other techniques you can use. You may also wish to share information before reading in the following ways:

- Show a picture that illustrates the concept or time period, or sets the scene.
- Read a section from a book that explains the necessary prior knowledge.
- List key facts on the board and discuss them with students.

When students use prereading tools (such as a Smart Chart), prior knowledge is activated, helping them create a framework on which to hang new knowledge (Graves, Juel, & Graves, 1998).

SAMPLE SMART CHART
Selection: *The Louisiana Purchase*

Background B	What We Know K	What We Want to Know W	What We Learned L
The western boundary of the U.S. in 1800 was the Mississippi River. U.S. hunters, trappers, and other pioneers were pushing westward into the wilderness past the Mississippi. Much of this land was owned by France and Spain. However it was populated by many Indian Nations. France was engaged in a war with Great Britain and needed money to support the war effort.	In 1803 Louisiana was not yet a state. It was part of the Louisiana Territory, owned by France. Thomas Jefferson was president of the U.S. in 1803. The U.S. had fewer states in 1803 than it does today.	Why was it called the Louisiana Purchase? Whom did we buy it from? How much did it cost? How big was the Louisiana Purchase?	Jefferson bought the Louisiana Territory from France in 1803 for $15 million. It doubled the size of the U.S. Lewis and Clark explored the territory for the U.S. government. Sacajawea, their Shoshone guide, helped them navigate the land and waterways. France called this territory Louisiana after their king, Louis.

To use a Smart Chart, follow the four steps as modeled in this classroom snapshot below:

Setting: *Mrs. G. teaches fifth grade. Her class is reading a selection about the Louisiana Purchase. She displays the chart and says: "Today we are going to read a selection called 'The Country Doubles Its Size.' This selection is about Thomas Jefferson's purchase of the Louisiana Territory in 1803."*

SAMPLE SMART CHART ROUTINE	
Routine	**Lesson Model**
1. Look for ways to build on and connect to student ideas when they share what they know. This is an ideal time to dispel misconceptions and correct inaccuracies. Student prior knowledge goes in the "What We Know" section. This is column head "K."	**Damien:** I know that Thomas Jefferson was a president. **Teacher:** That's right. He was the third president of the United States. **Emily:** I know that Louisiana is a state. **Teacher:** Excellent. But, in 1803 Louisiana wasn't a state yet. The United States only went as far west as the Mississippi River. Maybe we'll read why it was called the Louisiana Territory.
2. Based on gaps in students' prior knowledge, explain what they need to know so they can build "mental models," or pictures in their heads. This information goes in the background section. This is column head "B." You will fill this out with students as you present the information that they have not already shared but need to know.	*Teacher and students fill this out before reading.*
3. Use the "What We Want to Know" column to help students set a purpose for reading and to build their curiosity. This is column head "W."	**Emily:** Why was it called the Louisiana Purchase? **Miguel:** Who did we buy it from? **Damien:** And how much did it cost? **Midori:** How big was the Louisiana Purchase?
4. Use the "What We Learned" column to review important concepts in the text. This is column head "L."	*Teacher and students fill this out after reading as a summary of their learning. Students explain how and where they got the information.*

Remember, the goal is to provide a support for students on which to hang the information they will read. You are not summarizing, preteaching, or outlining what they will read prior to reading. If the information is not in the text but is necessary to understand the text, it needs to be pretaught.

PREVIEWING THE TEXT

An activity that will be extremely helpful to students before they begin to read a selection is previewing the text. A preview informs students about the content of the material and gives them a framework for reading. Anticipating what they are going to read about will alert them to important information.

Use the Let's Navigate activity (page 106 of this book) as you introduce the routine below. Continue to quickly walk through the basic steps before students begin reading other selections so that previewing the text becomes an automatic prereading strategy.

PREVIEW ROUTINE	
Routine	**Lesson Model**
1. Have students read the title of the selection, the introduction if there is one, and browse the photos or illustrations. Write students' responses on chart paper.	**Teacher:** Based on the title [and introduction], what do you think this article will be about?
2. Have students read each heading. Record each heading.	**Teacher:** What do you expect to read about in this section?
3. Have each student complete a prediction statement. Record a sampling of student predictions on the chart.	**Student:** I think this selection will be about _____. I decided this from the title, the headings, and what I already know about the topic.
4. After students complete the reading, have them verify their predictions.	Students confirm their predictions.
5. Restate the title and point out the introduction. Restate the headings.	**Teacher:** You can see that the title and introduction told you the main idea of the selection. Each heading was the main idea of the section that followed. These features clued you in to what to expect. They got you ready for the information in the selection that you were about to read.

PRETEACHING VOCABULARY

As you know from your own classroom experience, one of the many challenges facing students in their content area reading is vocabulary. Given the level of difficulty and the number of unfamiliar words that students are likely to encounter in a single chapter, you'll need to make some choices. One will be which words to teach. Another will be how to teach them.

Research shows that the direct teaching of vocabulary can help improve comprehension when we follow these guidelines (Cooper, 1993):

- **Teach a limited number of critical words at a time.** Limit the number of words to five or six and be sure that they are key to the main ideas in the text.

- **Teach the words in a meaningful context.** The context should reflect the particular meaning of the word in the text.

- **Help students relate the new words to their background knowledge.** Students are more likely to remember words linked to other concepts and words they already know.

- **Expose students to the words multiple times.** Students do not master new words after one presentation. Words have to be used in a variety of situations, including speaking and writing, before students "own" them.

Here's a simple routine we have used with our students to introduce and teach new vocabulary (Carnine et al., 1997).

VOCABULARY ROUTINE	
Routine	**Lesson Model**
1. Use a visual, such as a picture/photo in the text to be read.	**Teacher:** This is a statue of a pharaoh.
2. Model the pronunciation of the word.	*Teacher writes the word* pharaoh *on the chalkboard.* Teacher: This word is FA-roh. You say it.
3. Provide a synonym or a definition for each word. One way to define a word is to tell its class and then specify characteristics that make the word different from others in the same class.	**Teacher:** A pharaoh was a king in ancient Egypt. The rulers of other countries had different titles. In England, the title is king or queen. In China and Japan, the ruler was called an emperor or empress. A ruler in India was called a rajah.
4. Check students' understanding.	**Teacher:** What is a pharaoh? **Student:** A pharaoh is what a king was called in ancient Egypt.
5. Give examples and non-examples. Students tell whether or not the example illustrates the definition of the word and explain why or why not.	**Teacher:** Was King Tut a pharaoh? **Student:** Yes, he was a king of ancient Egypt. **Teacher:** What about King George II? Was he a pharaoh? **Student:** No. **Teacher:** Why not? **Student:** Because he was a king of England. **Teacher:** Does Egypt still have a pharaoh? **Student:** No, not anymore.
6. Provide vocabulary activities so that students may review the words and their definitions.	These activities include cloze sentences, matching words with definitions, and so on.

RETELLINGS

What Are They?

Retellings are oral or written recalls of text that students have read or heard read aloud. Retellings are often confused with summaries. When students retell, they are encouraged to include as much information as possible, not just the main points of the text. Summaries, on the other hand, focus on the main idea of the text and important supporting details. Retellings are, in fact, an important precursor to the development of summarization skills (Moss, 2004).

Why Are They Useful?

For students, retellings improve their understanding of a text and of text forms and conventions. They must organize the information they read, make inferences, relate the text to their personal experiences, and evaluate what was read (CORE, 1999). To accomplish these tasks, students interact with the text frequently and, with each rereading, in greater depth.

For you, retellings provide insights about a student's comprehension, depth of understanding, and ability to organize information. Retellings allow you to see *how well* as well as *how much* information students retain after reading or hearing a text (Moss, 2004).

By retelling expository text, students begin to intuit the text structure and organizational patterns used by the author. The greater students' awareness of these patterns is, the better their comprehension and retention of the information.

How Are They Introduced?

Children learn to recognize the elements of story structure—who the characters are, what happens to them, how the story ends—even before they start school. By the time children reach third grade, most of them are well versed in story structure and can identify its elements. The goal is to give children the same facility with nonfiction.

Children should be exposed to expository text structures as early as kindergarten. These early beginnings will result in students becoming increasingly familiar with expository patterns and more sophisticated in recognizing and using them while moving up through the grades. Each text structure should be taught individually and mastered before another is introduced. Begin with the structures that are more easily grasped—sequence and compare/contrast—and then move on to the more challenging ones, such as description, problem/solution, and cause/effect (Moss, 2004).

How Are They Taught?

Retellings of texts that illustrate a particular structure give students the opportunity to practice and apply their understanding of that structure. The two-phase sequence that follows, developed by Barbara Moss, can facilitate the development of students' retelling skills with expository text.

Phase 1 provides teacher modeling and scaffolding to enable students to develop an understanding of the retelling process.

Phase 2 provides students with opportunities for practice, first in large-group retellings and then, as skills increase, in small groups or pairs.

Phase 1: Teacher Models Retelling	Phase 2: Students Practice Retelling
Model by first using books with the more accessible structures such as sequence or compare/contrast. Then move on to more complex structures such as cause/effect or problem/solution. With younger children, use a Read Aloud. Older students may read the text on their own before you model retelling.	*Give students opportunities to practice first in large-group retellings and later in small groups or pairs.*
1. **Before reading a text**, activate prior knowledge and stimulate thinking about the content of the book. Use props or pictures to make the book concepts more concrete.	1. **Before reading a text**, activate prior knowledge. Encourage students to predict what the book will be about and what the text structure might be. Their answers may be based on the title, a preview of the book, and/or the table of contents.
2. **During reading of the text,** point out text features, such as signal words, headings, boldfaced words, and diagrams, that will aid in retelling. Instruct students to read or listen carefully to remember as much of the text as they can.	2. **After reading,** ask students what they remember about the text. Aid their recall with prompts such as: What did you find out first? What did you learn next? Can you tell me more? What else do you remember? Record students' responses.
3. **After reading,** model retelling the text as completely as possible. Involve students by asking them to add any missing information. Model "look backs" by rereading or directing students to reread specific parts of the text.	3. Reread the text or ask students to reread to identify missed information. Add to the information previously recorded. Use these and other questions: ● When you reread the text, how did you read it differently? ● What did you notice when you reread that you didn't notice the first time? ● How did rereading help you better understand the text?
4. **Model more "embellished" retellings,** by including personal anecdotes and analogies. Having students make the text their own is both acceptable and desirable.	4. Encourage students to make personal connections to the text. Record these as appropriate.

For more details, see: Moss, Barbara. Teaching Expository Text Structures Through Information Trade Book Retellings. *The Reading Teacher,* Vol. 57, No. 8, May 2004.

WRITING

Paragraph writing frames are an excellent way to scaffold student writing of expository text [Armbruster, Anderson, & Ostertag's study (as cited in Moss, 2003)].

- These frames are equally effective with young children or older students who struggle with writing.

- Originally designed for use with textbook material, the frames are equally useful with nonfiction trade books or magazine and newspaper articles.

- These frames help students to further their understanding of the most frequently encountered expository text patterns, which include description, sequence, compare/contrast, cause/effect, and problem/solution.

- Paragraph writing frames employ the cloze procedure, providing sentence starters that include signal words or phrases.

- When these frames are completed, students have written a paragraph that follows one of the most commonly used expository text structures.

- After learning about each expository text pattern through these strategies, students can then try their hand at writing paragraphs illustrating each pattern.

WRITING ROUTINE (Barbara Moss, 2003)
1. Introduce the various frames (opposite page) one at a time. First model the writing of a sample paragraph illustrating the organizational pattern being introduced. For example, write a paragraph about a topic that illustrates sequence. In this paragraph use signal words like *first, next, then*, and *finally*.
2. After that, review the sequence of events in the paragraph with each group.
3. Give students the sentences on sentence strips and have them arrange the sentences in order.
4. Students then copy the strips in paragraph form onto their papers.
5. Introduce the frame to the large group and fill it with students' responses. (It may help students if you provide the first sentence of the frame.)

Paragraph Writing Frames

Armbruster et al.'s study (as cited in Moss, 2003).

Description

_____ have many interesting features. First, they have _____, which allow them to _____. Second, they have _____, which are _____. Last they have _____, which _____.

Sequence

The first step in making a _____ is to _____. After that, you must _____. Thirdly, you need to _____. Finally, you _____.

Compare/Contrast

Both _____ and _____ are similar in many ways. They are similar because _____. They are also similar because _____. In some ways, though, _____ and _____ are different. They are different because _____ is _____. So, _____ and _____ have both similarities and differences.

Cause/Effect

Because of _____, _____ happened. Therefore, _____. This explains why _____.

Problem/Solution

The problem was that _____. This problem happened because _____. The problem was finally solved when _____.

LESSON 1 Reading Nonfiction

When faced with a typical page of nonfiction, many students feel bombarded and at a loss for how to navigate the page. Sophisticated readers may cruise whichever features first catch the eye before delving into the main text. Readers who are not as comfortable with nonfiction, however, need to be given a definite plan for how to proceed.

Unlike narrative text, nonfiction usually consists of a main article plus many additional features on the same page. The added information provides readers with support for the main article as well as supplementary facts related to the topic.

• **Photos** provide visual support for the text, as well as adding information for the viewer who knows how to look for it.

• **Captions** describe the photo, but they, too, usually add new information not presented in the main text.

• **Sidebars** are off to the side of the main article or sometimes below it.

• Readers have to consolidate all the information from the various features to get the whole picture.

TEACH

• Ask students to turn to **Student WorkText, page 4.**

• Have students read the page silently before discussing together steps for navigating the page, the sample article, and the added information.

TEACHER THINK ALOUD There is a lot happening on this page, isn't there? It's hard to know where to start reading. Let me show you how I navigate a page like this. You already know that you start by previewing the page to get yourself ready for what you're going to read. So the first thing I do is read the title and the introduction. I look at the photos, too, because they catch my eye. But I know that I'll come back and study them later on. I also notice that there is a sidebar, but I'm going to read that last.

The next thing I do is read the main article. Then I look at the article's photo carefully. It shows what I read about in the main article, but I know it can tell me more. The photo on this page shows me that a penguin can be totally covered in oil from a spill. The caption tells me something that wasn't in the article, too—that there was an oil spill near South Africa. Now I know that oil spills can happen in many different places in the world.

The last thing I do is read the sidebar. It's not about oil spills. It's about different kinds of penguins. Now I know even more interesting information about penguins!

• Have students follow the directions and answer the questions under *Practice Your Skills*. Check their answers and assist them, as needed, in reading the added information.

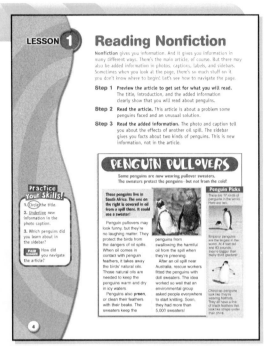

PRACTICE

- Ask students to turn to **Student WorkText, page 5**. Have them preview the article and complete the *Before You Read* prompt. (See **Preview Routine, page 20**.)

- Ask students to read the article silently. They will have an opportunity to retell at the end of the lesson. Then have students answer the *As You Read* questions on their own.

- Discuss the article using the *After You Read* questions.

 Have students model aloud how they navigated the page. Use the following prompts, as needed:

✔ What did you read first? next? last?

✔ How is the sidebar different from the rest of the page?

- Have volunteers share their pair-share discussions with the class.

Retelling Model retelling the text. Involve students by having them add one or two of the details. If needed, demonstrate "look backs" by rereading aloud particular parts of the article to refresh students' memories. *I am going to retell the selection, but I'm going to leave out one or two important details. Listen closely and tell me what else I should add.*

APPLY

- Ask students to turn to **Student WorkText, page 6**.

- Have students read the sidebar, and then draw and caption an illustration.

- You may wish to spark discussion with these and other questions:

✔ What did you already know about this topic?

✔ What new information did you learn from the sidebar?

✔ What new information did your drawing and caption add? **NAEP**

LESSON **2** · Reading Nonfiction

Whenever students read nonfiction, particularly social studies and science textbooks, have them navigate the text using the strategies they have learned. Encourage students to verbalize how they navigate next in order to internalize these strategies. Model as needed.

TEACH

- Ask students to turn to **Student WorkText, page 7**.

- Have students read the page silently before discussing together steps for navigating the page, the sample article, and the added information.

TEACHER THINK ALOUD You already know a lot about how to navigate a page of nonfiction. Let me quickly go over with you how I go about tackling this page. I start, as always, with a preview to get me set for what I'm going to read about. The title and headings tell me that the article is going to be about a new museum. And the photo shows me that it has something to do with Native Americans. I see there's a really interesting looking sidebar. I'll be sure to read it before I turn the page.

After my preview, I read the article. I was right. This is about a new museum that shows the history and art of different groups of Native Americans. Now I'll look at the photo carefully and read the caption. I can see that some tribes wore traditional clothing made with feathers. The article didn't mention that, but the photo shows it. Last, I read the sidebar. It tells me about artifacts made by different tribes.

I learned from all the information on this page that the new museum will teach people about how different American Indian tribes lived in the past and how they live today.

- Have students follow the directions and answer the question under *Practice Your Skills*. Check their answers and assist them, as needed, in navigating the page and reading the text.

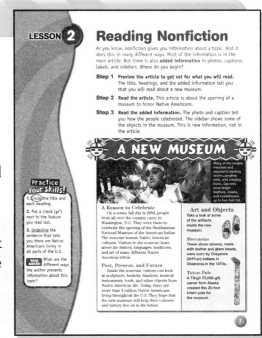

- Ask students to turn to **Student WorkText, page 8**. Have them preview the article and complete the *Before You Read* prompt. (See **Preview Routine, page 20**.)

- Ask students to read the article silently. Then have students answer the *As You Read* questions.

Have students model aloud how they navigated the page. Use the following prompts, as needed:

✔ What did you read first? next? last?

✔ How is the sidebar different from the rest of the page?

✔ What new information did you learn from the photos? from the captions?

- Discuss the article and added information features using the *After You Read* questions as a starting point. You may also wish to ask: *What are some of the ways the author presents information on this topic?*

- Have volunteers share their pair-share discussions with the class.

Retelling Model retelling the text. Involve students by having them add one or two of the details. If needed, demonstrate "look backs" by rereading aloud particular parts of the article to refresh students' memories.

APPLY

- Ask students to turn to **Student WorkText, page 9**. Have them complete the sentences before reading the article.

- Provide time for students to share their responses with the class.

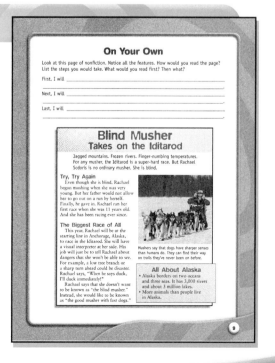

Problem/Solution

TEACH

Text Structure: Problem/Solution

- Discuss the importance of identifying how a text is structured. Tell students that figuring out how a selection is structured will help them organize their thinking as they read. Explain that a writer often uses signal words as clues to what the text structure is. Display the **Text Structures Poster**. (See **Student WorkText, page 105**.)

> **TEACHER THINK ALOUD** I know that writers organize their writing in a way that helps us better understand and remember the information. Let me show you how I figure out how the information in "Kid Inventors" is organized.
>
> The very first sentence of Bat Boy tells me that Jacob forgot his baseball. Well, I know that's going to be a problem if he wants to play ball! In the very next sentence I read the words *his problem*, so I know I'm right. An article that tells about a problem usually goes on to explain the solution to the problem. As I continue to read, I'm going to look for what Jacob's solution was. The article says that the problem gave Jacob an idea for an invention. The invention is the solution to the problem. That makes sense—people usually invent things to solve a problem.
>
> What about signal words? The words *therefore* and *as a result* are more clues that the text structure of the article is problem and solution.

Build Background: Smart Chart

- Use the **Smart Chart Routine, page 19**. Through your questioning, guide the discussion to identify students' knowledge and/or misconceptions about inventors and inventions.

Preteach Vocabulary

- Define each of the following words from "Kid Inventors." Provide a context sentence and point out that the three words are related; they have the same base word. (See **Vocabulary Routine, page 21**.)

invent   To think up and invent something new. *The Wright brothers invented the airplane.*

inventor   A person who invents or creates something new. *Thomas Edison was the inventor of the light bulb, the phonograph, and the movie projector.*

invention   Something new that has not been seen before. *The computer is an invention that has changed the way we live and work.*

- Ask students to turn to **Student WorkText, pages 10–11.** Direct their attention to *Before You Read*. Then have students use the words to fill in the chart. Students may use the names of inventors and inventions, as well as the words with inflected endings.

Person	Action	Thing
inventor	*invent*	*invention*
Additional answers may include:	*Additional answers may include:*	*Additional answers may include:*
inventors, Edison, A.G. Bell, Wright brothers	*invents, invented, inventing, create, originate*	*inventions, TV, DVD, compact disc, refrigerator, contact lenses*

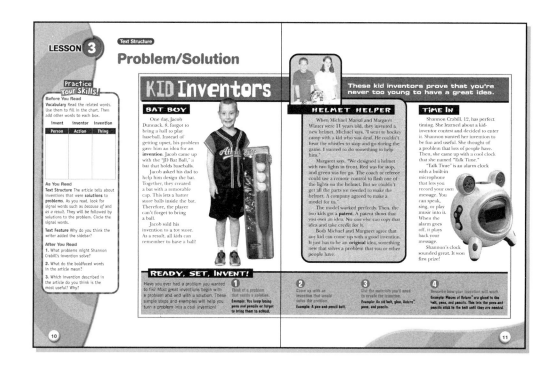

Read the Article

- Read aloud the *As You Read* text to help students set a purpose for reading. Then, ask students to read the article silently, paying special attention to the way they navigate the text and read the added information.

- When students have finished reading, discuss the article and added information using the *After You Read* questions.

Check Comprehension

- Have students retell the selection in their own words. Encourage them to include as many details from the article as they can recall. (See pages 21–23 for a detailed discussion of retellings.)

- You may wish to continue the discussion with these and other questions:
  - ✔ What qualities did the kid inventors have in common?
  - ✔ Why does an inventor get a patent?
  - ✔ What can you think of in everyday life that an invention would improve?
  - ✔ What did the author do to present the information clearly? **NAEP**

Graphic Organizer

- Ask students to turn to **Student WorkText, page 12.**

- Have them reread the article to determine any information left out of their retellings. Then ask students to complete the graphic organizer.

- When finished, have students do a second retelling to a partner.

- Use a graphic organizer such as this when students encounter problem/solution paragraphs in their social studies and science textbooks.

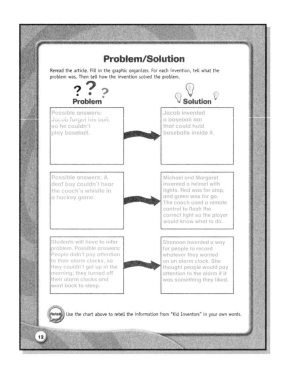

APPLY

Writing Frame

● Ask students to turn to **Student WorkText, page 13**.

● Have students complete the problem/solution writing frame using the information in the article on pages 10–11. Work with students, as needed.

On Your Own

● Have students write their own problem/solution paragraphs using information about inventors and inventions from their science textbook.

● Explain to students that the more practice they have using the problem/solution writing frame, the more familiar they will be with this text structure. This will assist them in recognizing the problem/solution pattern as they read, inform them about how to organize their thinking about their reading, and improve their reading comprehension overall. These writing frames can also be used when they answer test questions or write reports for social studies and science assignments.

Writing Frame

Use the information in your graphic organizer to fill in the writing frame.

Most inventions solve problems. Here are some examples.

One problem was that a kid could forget his or her ball and not be able to play baseball. This problem was solved when Jacob invented a baseball bat that can hold balls inside it

Another problem was that a deaf player could not hear the coach's whistle in a hockey game, so the player didn't know when to stop and when to go. This problem was solved when Michael and Margaret invented a helmet that has a red light and a green light. The coach controls the lights, so the player knows what to do

Another problem was that people don't always pay attention to their alarm clocks, so they get up late. This problem was solved when Shannon invented an alarm clock in which people can record whatever they want to wake up to

Use the writing frame above as a model to write a paragraph about another invention that solved a problem. Look in your science book if you need facts about inventors and their inventions.

13

LESSON 4 Nonfiction Features

Nonfiction features help readers understand science articles. They are added by the authors to make complex material easier to understand and remember.

- The chapter or article **title** tells what the topic is.

- The **introduction** and **headings** alert readers to the main ideas of the article.

- **Graphic aids**, such as charts, photographs, and diagrams, make the text more interesting and make the information easier to access and visualize.

- **Boldfaced words** highlight important vocabulary.

- **Pronunciation guides** help in pronouncing difficult or unusual words.

- **Sidebars**—which may contain maps, diagrams, charts, or facts—relate to the text and add information about the topic.

TEACH

- Ask students to turn to **Student WorkText, page 14**.

- Have students read the page silently before discussing together the sample article and how to read it.

 This article has a lot of things in it. At first glance, I see a large picture, text, headings, and words in bold. Wow! Where should I start? I have to figure out how I will navigate the text.

First, I will read the title. It tells me that this is an article about the heart. So, I think about what I already know about the heart, how it works, and why it's important to the body. This helps me relate the new information in the article to what I already know. That will make it easier to understand.

Then, I will read the introduction. It prepares me for what I will read in the article; it tells me the "big ideas."

Next, I will read the headings. These headings—heart, arteries, and veins—tell me that the article will be about how the heart works. That helps me organize my thinking as I read and helps me understand the big diagram in the middle of the page.

So, then I can read the main article. I will save all the sidebar information for the end. I'll read the sidebar information after I read the main text and then think about how this information relates to the big ideas in the article.

- Have students follow the directions and answer the questions under *Practice Your Skills*. Check their answers and assist them, as needed, in understanding the article.

PRACTICE

- Ask students to turn to **Student WorkText, page 15.** Have them preview the article and complete the *Before You Read* prompt. (See **Preview Routine, page 20.**)

- Ask students to read the article silently, paying special attention to the text features. Then have students answer the *As You Read* questions.

STUDENT THINK ALOUD   Have students model aloud how they read the article. Use the following prompts, as needed:

✔ How did you navigate the article? What did you read first? last?

✔ Why is the main photo included?

✔ What information does the sidebar provide?

- Discuss the article using the *After You Read* questions.

- Have volunteers share their pair-share discussions.

Retelling   Model retelling the text. Involve students by having them add one or two of the details. If needed, demonstrate "look backs" by rereading aloud particular parts of the article to refresh students' memories.

APPLY

- Ask students to turn to **Student WorkText, page 16.**

- Have students read the article and then supply the missing text features. Before they begin, discuss with students the function of each of the text features.

- Then ask students to trade papers with a partner and review each other's work. Provide time for students to share their answers.

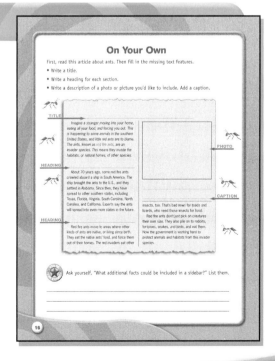

LESSON 5 Nonfiction Features

TEACH

- Ask students to turn to **Student WorkText, page 17**.

- Have students read the page silently before discussing together the sample article and steps for reading it.

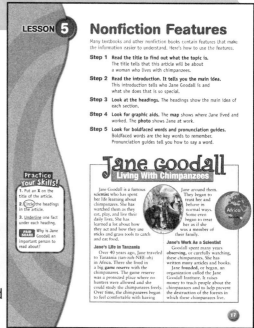

TEACHER THINK ALOUD This article has a lot of things in it, too. At first glance, I see a map, a photo, text, headings, and words in bold. So . . . where should I start? I need to figure out how I will navigate the text.

First, I will read the title. It tells me that this is an article about a woman named Jane Goodall who lives with chimps. That sounds interesting. I need to think if I've ever heard of Jane Goodall or about someone who lives with chimps. I once saw a TV program about a lady who studied monkeys. Maybe that was Jane Goodall?

Then, I'll read the introduction. It prepares me for what I will read in the article; it tells me the "big ideas."

Next, I'll read the headings. The headings tell me that I will read about Jane's life in Tanzania and her work as a scientist. Now I know that she lives with chimps because she studies them. That makes sense. She does this work in Tanzania. When I look on the map, I see that Tanzania is in Africa. A lot of chimps live there.

This information will help me organize my thinking as I read. Then I'll be able to read the main article. The article will give me more details about this interesting woman and her work.

- Have students follow the directions and answer the question under *Practice Your Skills*. Check their answers and assist them, as needed, in noticing and reading the text features.

PRACTICE

- Ask students to turn to **Student WorkText, page 18**. Have students preview the article and complete the *Before You Read* prompt. (See **Preview Routine, page 20**.)

- Ask students to read the article silently, paying special attention to the text features. Then have students answer the *As You Read* questions.

THINK ALOUD Have students model aloud how they read the article containing multiple text features. Use the following prompts, as needed:

✔ What did you read first?

✔ Where did you look to find the main ideas of the article?

✔ How does the information in the map and photos add to or illustrate the information in the article? **NAEP**

- Discuss the article and text features using the *After You Read* questions as a starting point. You may also wish to ask: *Where can you find additional information about the topics covered in the article?*

- Have volunteers share their pair-share discussion with the class.

Retelling Model retelling the text. Involve students by having them add one or two of the details.

APPLY

- Ask students to turn to **Student WorkText, page 19**.

- Have students read the article and then supply the missing text features.

- You may wish to spark discussion about the article with these and other questions:

✔ What does an author do to organize the information clearly? **NAEP**

✔ What photo or sidebar would you add to this article? Why?

- Then have students complete *You Be the Expert!* Students will write questions about the article for classmates to answer.

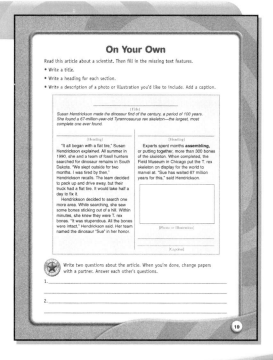

TEACH

Text Structure: Compare/Contrast

● Discuss the importance of identifying how a text is structured. Tell students that figuring out how a selection is structured will help them organize their thinking as they read. Explain that a writer often uses signal words as clues to what the text structure is. Display the **Text Structures Poster**. (See **Student WorkText, page 105**.)

> **TEACHER THINK ALOUD** I know that writers organize their writing in a way that helps us better understand and remember the information. In the article "Dino Time" the writer compares and contrasts dinosaur discoveries in Madagascar and Argentina.
>
> As I read, I will look for how these discoveries are the same and how they are different. This will help me organize my thinking as I read. I'll look for clue words that help me. Words such as *bigger, oldest,* and *largest* show comparison. I already see some of these words in the headings, so I know they will be useful as I read.

Build Background: Smart Chart

● Use the **Smart Chart Routine, page 19**. Through your questioning, guide the discussion to identify students' knowledge and/or misconceptions about dinosaurs.

Preteach Vocabulary

● Define each of the following words from "Dino Time." Provide a context sentence and point out any related words. (See **Vocabulary Routine, page 21**.)

extinct   A plant or animal that has died out. *The dodo bird was a large bird that became extinct in the 1700s.*
Related words: *extinction*

expert   Someone who is very skilled at something or knows a lot about a particular subject. *That scientist was an expert on dinosaurs.*
Related word: *expertise*

species A group of animals that share the same characteristics and can mate and have offspring. *The scientist found a new species of bird in the rain forest.*

existed Lived. *Dinosaurs existed a long time ago.*

discovered Found. *The scientist also discovered a new kind of flower in the rain forest.*

● Ask students to turn to **Student WorkText, pages 20–21**. Direct their attention to *Before You Read* and have them complete the Related Word Pairs activity before they begin to read the article.

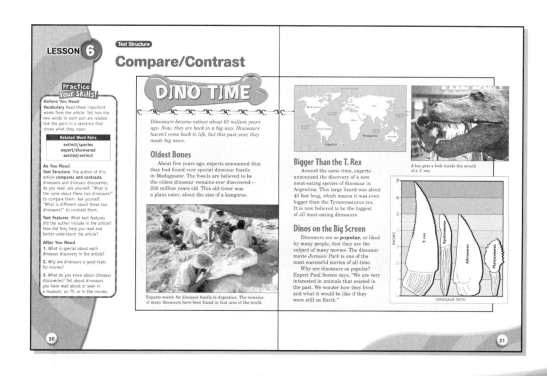

Read the Article

● Read aloud the *As You Read* text to help students set a purpose for reading. Then, ask students to read the article silently, paying special attention to the headings, map, and graph.

Check Comprehension

● Have students retell the selection in their own words. Encourage them to include as many details from the article as they can recall. (See pages 21–23 for a detailed discussion of retelling.)

● When students have finished reading, discuss the article using the *After You Read* questions.

● You may wish to continue the discussion with these and other questions:

✔ Where was a new meat-eating dinosaur found? What makes it so special?

✔ What information does the map provide? How does it relate to the article?

✔ How did the headings help you organize your thinking as you read? How did they help you in your retellings?

Graphic Organizer

● Ask students to turn to **Student WorkText, page 22.**

● Have them reread the article to determine any information left out of their retellings. Then ask students to complete the graphic organizer.

● When finished, have students do a second retelling to a partner.

● Use a graphic organizer such as a Venn diagram whenever students encounter compare/contrast paragraphs in their social studies and science textbooks.

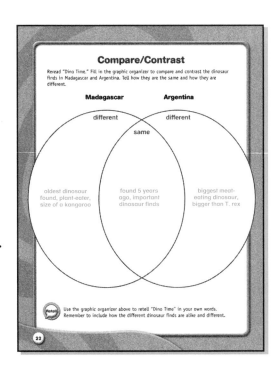

APPLY

Writing Frame

- Ask students to turn to **Student WorkText, page 23**.

- Remind students that writers use certain words and phrases when writing compare/contrast paragraphs. These include *both, same, different, so, therefore, but, unlike, however,* and *in contrast to*. These words and phrases are called *signal words*. They signal that the author is comparing or contrasting information. This helps readers organize their thinking about the text. When comparing and contrasting, authors also use comparative words ending in *-er* and *-est*.

On Your Own

- Have students write their own compare/contrast paragraph using information from their science textbook. Students will compare and contrast two types of animals, such as two species.

- Explain to students that the more practice they have using the compare/contrast writing frame, the more familiar they will be with this text structure. This will assist them in recognizing the compare/contrast pattern as they read, inform them about how to organize their thinking about their reading and writing, and improve their reading comprehension overall.

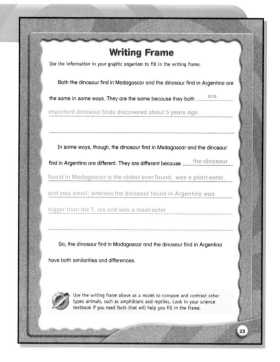

Writing Frame

Use the information in your graphic organizer to fill in the writing frame.

Both the dinosaur find in Madagascar and the dinosaur find in Argentina are the same in some ways. They are the same because they both _____ are important dinosaur finds discovered about 5 years ago

In some ways, though, the dinosaur find in Madagascar and the dinosaur find in Argentina are different. They are different because _____ the dinosaur found in Madagascar is the oldest ever found, was a plant-eater, and was small; whereas the dinosaur found in Argentina was bigger than the T. rex and was a meat-eater

So, the dinosaur find in Madagascar and the dinosaur find in Argentina have both similarities and differences.

Use the writing frame above as a model to compare and contrast other types animals, such as amphibians and reptiles. Look in your science textbook if you need facts that will help you fill in the frame.

23

LESSON 7 Diagrams

A **diagram** is a picture that shows the parts of something or how something works. A diagram helps you "picture" information that you read and makes that information easier to understand. For example, a diagram in a common household manual can illustrate a complicated process, such as how to assemble a cabinet, and help make the text clear.

- Labels identify the important parts of a diagram. A line connects the label to the part of the diagram that is described.

- Diagrams may also contain arrows, numbers, or letters to indicate the order in which the information should be read.

TEACH

- Ask students to turn to **Student WorkText, page 24**.

- Have students read the page silently before discussing together the sample diagram and steps to read it.

TEACHER THINK ALOUD This picture is a diagram. It's a whole little scene! Let me show you how I figure out what it's all about. First, I'll read the title and the introduction to find out what the diagram shows. They tell me that this is a diagram of the underground homes in which gophers live. The introduction says that other animals also use the tunnels for safety. I can see them in the diagram.

Next, I'll read the labels. Some of the labels are words—like *Mount St. Helens* and *rocks and ash*—with arrows pointing to what they are naming. But other labels are captions that describe parts of the tunnel and how they are used.

In one of the captions, I see the key word *burrows* [point to word in text], in italics. That tells me it's an important word, so I have to be sure I know what it means. The sentence tells me that burrows are underground tunnels.

- Have students follow the directions and answer the questions under *Practice Your Skills*. Check their answers and assist them, as needed, in interpreting the diagram.

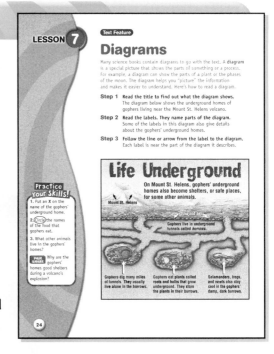

PRACTICE

- Ask students to turn to **Student WorkText, page 25.** Have them preview the article and complete the *Before You Read* prompt. (See **Preview Routine, page 20.**)

- Ask students to read the article silently, paying special attention to the diagram. Then have students answer the *As You Read* questions on their own.

 Have students model aloud how they read the diagram. Use the following prompts, as needed:

- ✔ What did you read first?
- ✔ How did you decide what to read next? after that?
- ✔ How do these labels differ from labels on other diagrams you have seen?

- Discuss the article and diagram using the *After You Read* questions. You may also wish to ask: *How could this diagram help someone who has never seen a volcano? What does this diagram teach you about volcanoes?*

- Have volunteers share their pair-share discussions.

Retelling Model retelling the text. Involve students by having them add one or two of the details.

APPLY

- Ask students to turn to **Student WorkText, page 26.**

- Have students study the diagrams in order to answer and write questions about their content. Before they begin, orally brainstorm sample questions with students.

- Have students complete the questions in *You Be the Expert!* Then ask students to trade papers with a partner and answer each other's questions. Provide time for all students to share their questions and answers with the whole class.

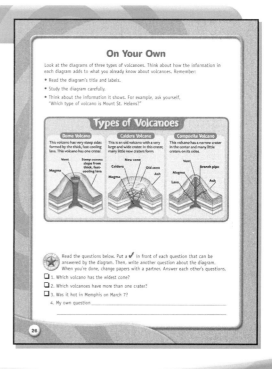

LESSON **8** Diagrams

CONNECTING TO YOUR CURRICULUM

Diagrams

You will find these and other diagrams in your social studies and science textbooks. Use these as opportunities to reinforce students' skills.

Social Studies

- a compass rose
- a map scale
- different types of communities
- the buildings in a U.S. city
- excavation site of U.S. settlement, such as Jamestown
- early invention

Science

- the water cycle
- the layers of Earth
- landforms in the United States
- parts of a plant
- parts of an animal
- different ecosystems
- sample food chain
- the phases of the moon
- the solar system
- how simple machines work

TEACH

- Ask students to turn to **Student WorkText, page 27.**
- Have students read the page silently before discussing together the sample diagram and steps for reading it.

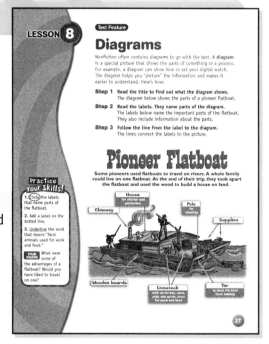

TEACHER THINK ALOUD Since we already talked about how to read science diagrams, let's look at this diagram together.

As you know, first we read the title to find out what the diagram is about. This diagram shows a flatboat, one of the methods of transportation early settlers used to travel up and down rivers.

Next, we read each label. The labels name the important parts of the flatboat, such as the wooden boards, house, and steering pole. They also show what was carried onboard. We follow the arrow from the label to the picture to see exactly which part of the flatboat is being identified.

We also remember to read the caption to see what information it adds.

- Have students follow the directions and answer the questions under *Practice Your Skills*. Check their answers and assist them, as needed, in interpreting the diagram.

PRACTICE

- Ask students to turn to **Student WorkText, page 28.** Have them preview the article and complete the *Before You Read* prompt. (See **Preview Routine, page 20.**)

- Ask students to read the article silently, paying special attention to the diagram. Then have students answer the *As You Read* questions on their own.

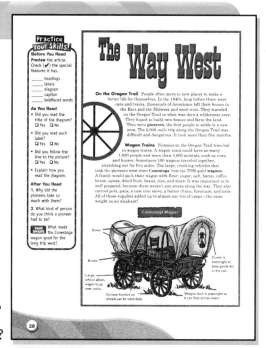

 Have students model aloud how they read the diagram. Use the following prompts, as needed:

✔ What did you read first?

✔ How did you find out about the parts of a Conestoga wagon?

✔ How can you tell which part of the wagon the label is naming?

- Discuss the article and diagram using the *After You Read* questions as a starting point. You may also wish to ask: *How does the information in the diagram help you understand the information in the article? What is special about the Conestoga wagon bed? the cover? the wheels?*

- Have volunteers share their pair-share discussion with the class.

Retelling Model retelling the text. Involve students by having them add one or two of the details.

APPLY

- Ask students to turn to **Student WorkText, page 29.** Have them complete the computer diagram. Discuss: *How could this diagram help someone who has never used a computer?*

- Then have students read *You Be the Expert!* and create their own diagrams.

- You may wish to spark discussion about the diagrams with these and other questions:

✔ How did you decide what was important to label?

✔ What additional information did you add to your labels? Why?

✔ Would someone be able to use the object you drew just by looking at your diagram? If not, what additional information would be needed?

Description

TEACH

Text Structure: Description

● Discuss the importance of identifying how a text is structured. Tell students that figuring out how a selection is structured will help them organize their thinking as they read. Explain that a writer often uses signal words as clues to what the text structure is. Display the **Text Structures Poster**. (See **Student WorkText, page 105**.)

> **TEACHER THINK ALOUD** I know that writers organize their writing in a way that helps us better understand and remember the information. In the article "Discover the Deep," the writer describes the three zones, or layers, of the ocean.
>
> As I read, I will look for the name of each zone and details that tell about what makes that zone different from other zones and which plants and animals live there. I'll look for clue words that help me. Words and phrases including *for example, like, such as*, and *another* are clues that the author is providing details about each ocean layer or ocean animal.

Build Background: Smart Chart

● Use the **Smart Chart Routine, page 19**. Through your questioning, guide the discussion to identify students' knowledge and/or misconceptions about oceans and ocean life.

Preteach Vocabulary

● Define each of the following words from "Discover the Deep." Provide a context sentence and point out any related words or useful word parts. (See **Vocabulary Routine, page 21**.)

prey Any animal that is hunted by another animal for food. *Tuna and other small fish are prey for larger sea animals such as sharks and whales. Prey* and *pray* are homophones.

zone   An area or layer, such as the ocean's zones and the earth's climate zones. *The top zone in the ocean is called the Sunlight Zone. Zone goes back to the Greek word meaning "belt," which is what zone once meant in English.*

● Ask students to turn to **Student WorkText, pages 30–31.** Direct their attention to *Before You Read.*

RELATED WORD PAIRS	
prey hunter	*antonyms*
zone layer	*synonyms*
prey pray	*homophones*

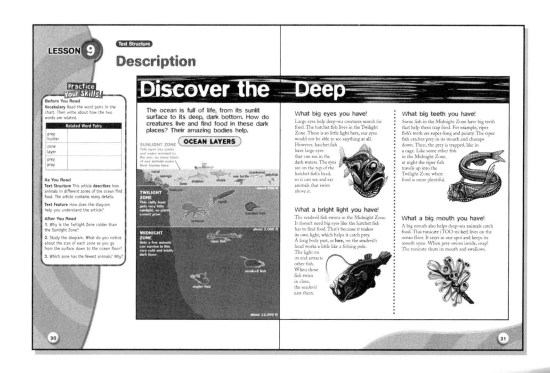

Read the Article

- Read aloud the *As You Read* text to help students set a purpose for reading. Then, ask students to read the article silently, paying special attention to the diagram.

- When students have finished reading, discuss the article and diagram using the *After You Read* questions.

Check Comprehension

- Have students retell the selection in their own words. Encourage them to include as many details from the article as they can recall. (See pages 21–23 for a detailed discussion of retellings.)

- You may wish to continue the discussion with these and other questions:

  ✔ Why is the Sunlight Zone the warmest? Why is the Midnight Zone the coldest?

  ✔ How do you think the Twilight Zone got its name?

  ✔ Which ocean animal in the article most interests you? Why?

  ✔ How did the information in the diagram help you understand the article? **NAEP**

Graphic Organizer

- Ask students to turn to **Student WorkText, page 32.**

- Have them reread the article to determine any information left out of their retellings. Then ask students to complete the graphic organizer to highlight the main ideas and supporting details.

- When finished, have students do a second retelling to a partner.

- Use a graphic organizer such as this whenever students encounter description paragraphs in their social studies and science textbooks.

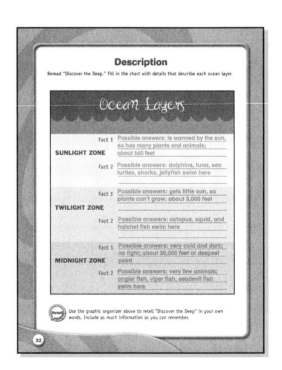

Writing Frame

- Ask students to turn to **Student WorkText, page 33**.

- Explain that writers use certain words and phrases when writing description paragraphs. These include *many, a few, like, such as,* and *is called*. These words and phrases are called *signal words*. They signal that the author is providing descriptive information, often in the form of supporting details. This helps readers organize their thinking about the text.

- Have students complete the description writing frame using the information in the article on pages 30–31. Work with students, as needed.

On Your Own

- Have students write their own description paragraph using information from their science textbook. Students will describe the layers in Earth's crust.

- Explain to students that the more practice they have using the description writing frame, the more familiar they will be with this text structure. This will assist them in recognizing the description pattern as they read, inform them about how to organize their thinking about their reading, and improve their overall reading comprehension. These writing frames can also be used when students answer test questions or write reports for social studies and science assignments.

Writing Frame

Use the information in your graphic organizer to fill in the writing frame.

The ocean has three zones, or layers. The top layer is called the
Sunlight Zone. This layer _is warmed by the sun._
Plants can grow here
Many animals, such as _tuna, dolphins, sea turtles, and sharks_
_____ swim here.
The middle layer is called the _Twilight Zone_
This layer _is chilly; doesn't get a lot of sunlight, so plants can't grow_
_____. A few animals,
such as _octopus, hatchet fish, and squid_ live here.
The bottom layer is called the _Midnight Zone_
This layer _is very cold and gets no light_
Very, very few animals, such as _angler fish, viper fish, and_
seadevil fish live here.

Use the writing frame above as a model to write a description of the layers in the Earth. Look in your science textbook if you need facts that will help you fill in the frame.

33

LESSON 10 · Special Type

One of the most obvious features that students will notice about nonfiction is how the text looks on the page. Writers of nonfiction provide visual "clues," such as **special type**, that alert readers to the important ideas and vocabulary central to the topic.

In expository text, these are among the organizational features that help students comprehend and remember what they read:

- The **title** and **headings** get students ready for what they are going to read. They provide an outline of the main ideas in the text.

- **Special type**, such as boldface, italics, pronunciations, and color, calls out important vocabulary related to the topic.

TEACH

- Ask students to turn to **Student WorkText, page 34**.

- Have students read the page silently before discussing together the sample text and steps for using the special type that appears in it.

 TEACHER THINK ALOUD Just one look at this page tells me it's not from a story! For one thing, there are so many different kinds of type. You may not realize it, but they are clues to help you better understand the text. Let me walk you through how to use these clues.

The title tells me that the article is about pets that become problems. The first heading tells me that the next section will be about pets that become problems because they get way too big. The second heading tells me that I will learn about why it's important to think before buying a pet. So as I read, I'll pay attention to what pets can be problems and why.

I also see words that are in boldface, or dark type. I can't miss them! The writer makes them stand out because they are important vocabulary about the topic. If the word is new to me, I'll make sure I learn what it means.

Then there is an odd-looking word in parentheses. Actually, it's not a word—it's a pronunciation. It tells me how to say the word just before it. *B-o-a* is pronounced (BOH-uh). In case I don't know how to say the word, the pronunciation is there to help me.

- Have students follow the directions and answer the questions under *Practice Your Skills*. Check their answers and assist them, as needed, in using the special type features.

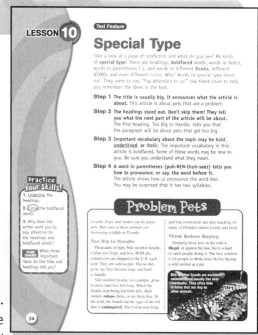

PRACTICE

- Ask students to turn to **Student WorkText, page 35.**
  Have them preview the article and complete the *Before
  You Read* prompt. (See **Preview Routine, page 20.**)

- Ask students to read the article silently, paying attention
  to the special type. Then have students answer the *As You
  Read* questions on their own.

STUDENT THINK ALOUD Have students model aloud how they used the
special type. Use the following prompts, as needed:

  ✔ What did you read first? What did that tell you?

  ✔ What did the headings tell you?

  ✔ Did you know the meanings of all the boldfaced words?
     If not, how did you figure them out?

- Discuss the article and special type using the *After You Read* questions.
  You may also wish to ask: *Does this article remind you of anything else
  we've read? How did that help you when you read this article?*

- Have volunteers share their pair-share discussions with the class.

Retelling Model retelling the text. Involve students by having them add
one or two of the details.

APPLY

- Ask students to turn to **Student WorkText, page 36.**

- You may wish to spark discussion with these and other
  questions:

  ✔ Which reptile fact surprised you the most?

  ✔ What are the ways the author presented information in
     this article? **NAEP**

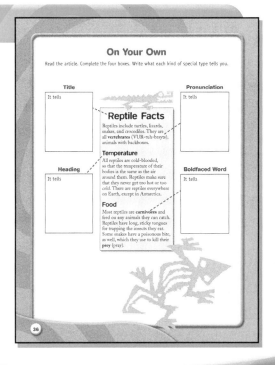

Special Type

You will find many examples of special type in your social studies and science textbooks. Use them as opportunities to reinforce students' skills.

Social Studies

- chapter titles in a large font and in color
- boldfaced section titles and headings
- pronunciations of proper nouns, foreign words, key vocabulary
- concept vocabulary in boldface
- special features called out in color

Science

- chapter titles in a large font and in color
- boldfaced section titles and headings
- pronunciations of technical terms and vocabulary
- concept vocabulary in boldface
- secondary vocabulary in italics
- special features called out in color

TEACH

- Ask students to turn to **Student WorkText, page 37**.
- Have students read the page silently before discussing together the sample article and the steps for using the special type that appears in it.

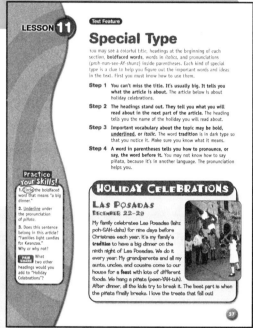

TEACHER THINK ALOUD Let me show you how I use the special type in this article. The title and heading get me ready for what I'm going to read. The title tells me the topic of the article—holiday celebrations. I wonder which holiday it's going to be about. Then I'll read the heading, and I'll know. I'll be learning about Las Posadas.

That's Spanish, and I'm not sure I'm pronouncing it correctly. But I see the pronunciation is given in the first sentence, so I can check. It's pronounced (lahz poh-SAH-dahz). I was pretty close!

In the second sentence, I come to a boldfaced word. That means it's an important word. I know what *tradition* means, but if I didn't, I could figure it out from the sentence *We do it every year*. The fact that *tradition* is boldfaced also gives me a clue that I'll be reading about what this family's traditions are.

As I continue to read, I'll be sure to use the other pronunciations and pay special attention to the boldfaced words.

- Have students follow the directions and answer the questions under *Practice Your Skills*. Check their answers and assist them, as needed, in using the special type.

PRACTICE

- Ask students to turn to **Student WorkText, page 38.** Direct students to *Before You Read*. Have them preview the article and respond. (See **Preview Routine, page 20.**)

- Ask students to read the article silently, paying attention to the special type. Have them answer the *As You Read* questions on their own.

 STUDENT THINK ALOUD Have students model aloud how they used the special type as they read. Use the following prompts, as needed:

- ✔ What did you read first? What did it tell you?

- ✔ Did you need any of the pronunciations? If so, which ones?

- ✔ Did you know the meaning of the word in boldfaced type? If not, what did you do to figure it out?

- Discuss students' answers. Then discuss the article and the special type that it contained using the *After You Read* questions. You may also wish to ask: *Did any of the information surprise you? How might these myths have started?*

Retelling Model retelling of the text. Involve students by having them add one or two details.

APPLY

- Ask students to turn to **Student WorkText, page 39.**
- Have students answer the questions in *You Be the Expert!*
- You may also wish to discuss:

  - ✔ How do you think we know about what Pilgrim life was like?

  - ✔ Would you like to be one of the Pilgrim children actors at Plimoth Plantation? Why or why not?

  - ✔ Why might the author have written this article? **NAEP**

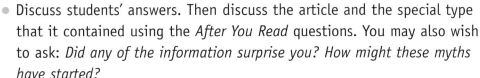

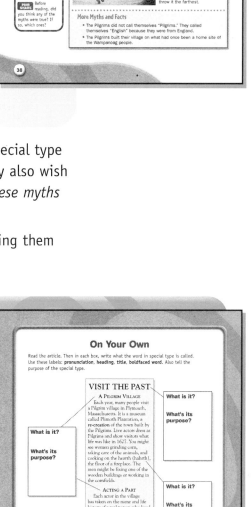

Cause/Effect

TEACH

Text Structure: Cause/Effect

● Remind students that writers of nonfiction often organize their writing in one of five ways: description, sequence, compare/contrast, cause/effect, problem/solution. Knowing how the writing is organized helps readers understand and remember what they read. Display the **Text Structures Poster**. (See **Student WorkText, page 105.**)

● The text structure of "It's Tornado Time" is cause/effect. You may wish to use the *Think Aloud* to model how you determined the text structure of the article.

TEACHER THINK ALOUD You know that figuring out how an article is organized can help you better understand the ideas in it. So, let me show you how I figured out the organization—or the text structure—of this article.

I know that writers use signal words to help me understand how the ideas are organized, so as I read I look for these clues. And I spot one in the first paragraph. It says that the family knew "the terrible effects of a tornado." I think the text structure of the article may be cause and effect. I'll continue reading to see if I'm right.

The next sentence says the family was safe. Why? "Because they were well prepared and remained calm." *Because* is another signal word. It tells me why the family was safe, or the cause of their being safe.

I see that the organization of this article is cause and effect. So as I read, I'll look for what happened and think about why it happened.

Build Background: Smart Chart

● Use the **Smart Chart Routine, page 19**. Through your questioning, guide the discussion to identify students' knowledge and/or misconceptions about tornadoes and their effects.

Preteach Vocabulary

● Define each of the following words from "It's Tornado Time." Provide a context sentence and point out any special features such as silent letters and homophones. (See **Vocabulary Routine, page 21.**)

destroy To ruin completely. *The tide destroyed the sandcastle.*

prepared Being ready for something. *Pat studied and was prepared for the test.*

calm Quiet, in control of oneself. *It is important to stay calm in an emergency.*

patience The ability to wait for something without getting upset or angry. *It's hard to have patience when you're waiting in a very long line.* Homophone: patients.

damage Harm, ruin, injury. *The bugs caused damage to many trees and plants.*

● Ask students to turn to **Student WorkText, pages 40–41**. Direct their attention to *Before You Read* and have them complete the chart before they begin to read the article.

WHAT'S THE CONNECTION?

		Synonym	Antonym
destroy	ruin	✓	
prepared	unprepared		✓
calm	upset		✓
patience	impatience		✓
damage	harm	✓	

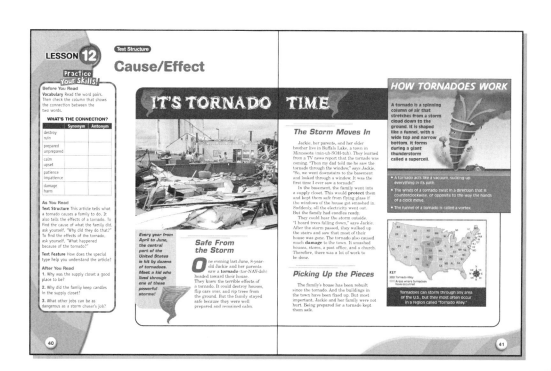

Read the Article

- Read aloud the *As You Read* text to help students set a purpose for reading. Then, ask students to read the article silently, paying attention to the special type.

- When students have finished reading, discuss the article and special type using the *After You Read* questions.

Check Comprehension

- Have students retell the selection in their own words. Encourage them to include as many details from the article as they can recall. (See pages 21–23 for a detailed discussion of retellings.)

- You may wish to continue the discussion with these and other questions:

  ✔ What are some of the effects of a tornado?

  ✔ Why was it important for the family to be well prepared?

  ✔ Have you and your family ever had to prepare for severe weather? If so, how?

  ✔ What clues did you find to help you figure out the cause/effect organization of the article? **NAEP**

Graphic Organizer

- Ask students to turn to **Student WorkText, page 42**.

- Have them reread the article to determine any information left out of their retellings. Then ask students to complete the graphic organizer.

- When finished, have students do a second retelling to a partner.

- Use a graphic organizer such as this whenever students encounter cause/effect paragraphs in their social studies and science textbooks.

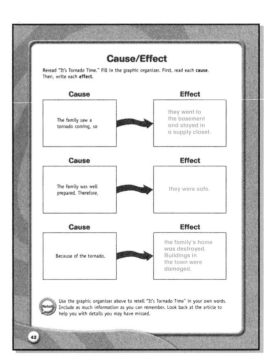

Cause/Effect

Reread "It's Tornado Time." Fill in the graphic organizer. First, read each **cause**. Then, write each **effect**.

Cause		Effect
The family saw a tornado coming, so	→	they went to the basement and stayed in a supply closet.
The family was well prepared. Therefore,	→	they were safe.
Because of the tornado.	→	the family's home was destroyed. Buildings in the town were damaged.

Use the graphic organizer above to retell "It's Tornado Time" in your own words. Include as much information as you can remember. Look back at the article to help you with details you may have missed.

42

Writing Frame

- Ask students to turn to **Student WorkText, page 43**.

- Explain that writers use certain words and phrases when writing about cause and effect. These include *because, so,* and *therefore*. These words and phrases are called *signal words*. They signal that the author is providing information about what happened and why. This helps readers organize their thinking about the text.

- Have students complete the cause/effect writing frame using the information in the article on pages 40–41. Work with students, as needed.

On Your Own

- Have students write their own cause/effect paragraphs using information from their science textbook.

- Explain to students that the more practice they have using the cause/effect writing frame, the more familiar they will be with this text structure. This will assist them in recognizing the cause/effect pattern as they read, inform them about how to organize their thinking about their reading, and improve their reading comprehension overall. These writing frames can also be used when they answer test questions or write reports for social studies and science assignments.

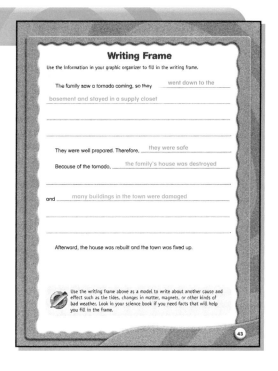

Writing Frame

Use the information in your graphic organizer to fill in the writing frame.

The family saw a tornado coming, so they _went down to the basement and stayed in a supply closet_

They were well prepared. Therefore, _they were safe_

Because of the tornado, _the family's house was destroyed_

and _many buildings in the town were damaged_

Afterward, the house was rebuilt and the town was fixed up.

Use the writing frame above as a model to write about another cause and effect such as the tides, changes in matter, magnets, or other kinds of bad weather. Look in your science book if you need facts that will help you fill in the frame.

LESSON 13 Flow Charts

A **flow chart** is a kind of diagram that shows a sequence of steps in a process.

- Some flow charts show a linear process, such as the production of bread. Others show a cyclical process, such as the life cycle of an animal.

- A flow chart shows in a visual format information that may require a long and complicated written explanation. The flow chart helps readers visualize the text, making the text easier to understand and remember.

- The information in a flow chart is arranged in sequential order.

TEACH

- Ask students to turn to **Student WorkText, page 44**.

- Have students read the page silently before discussing together the sample flow chart and steps for reading it.

TEACHER THINK ALOUD Let's talk about how to read this flow chart. First, I read the title, "From Corn to Cereal." That tells me that the flow chart will show how corn is made into cereal. I see that there are five steps. Each step has a number. That makes it easy for me—I just follow the numbers!

Of course I start reading at number 1. I look at the picture. Sometimes, if I don't know very much about the topic, I'm not too sure about what the picture shows. So I have to read the caption very carefully. When I'm finished, I follow the arrow and go on to step number 2. That way I'm reading each step in the right order.

When I finish reading the flow chart, I'll know how corn from the farm is made into a cereal I eat for breakfast!

- Have students follow the directions and answer the questions under *Practice Your Skills*. Check their answers and assist them, as needed, in reading the flow chart.

LESSON 13 — Text Feature

Flow Charts

Nonfiction may explain how something is made. Often, there is a diagram that shows each step in the process. The diagram is called a **flow chart**. It's important to follow the steps in the correct order. Otherwise, you might put the corn into boxes before it's made into flakes!

Step 1 Read the title. It tells you what the flow chart is about. The chart below shows how corn becomes corn flakes.

Step 2 Follow the numbers. They tell you the order of the steps. Always start at number 1. In this flow chart, arrows also point the way.

Step 3 Look at the illustration for each step and read the caption.

Step 4 Make sure you understand what happens in each step. Use the illustrations and captions to be sure you understand how corn is made into corn-flake cereal.

Practice Your Skills!

1. Underline the caption that tells what happens after the corn is toasted.

2. Circle the illustration that shows what happens last.

PAIR SHARE What are some steps you could add to the flow chart? Why do you think the flow chart doesn't show them?

From Corn to Cereal

Corn is sent from the farm to the factory.

The corn kernels are taken off the cobs and cooked. Then, the cooked corn is dried out.

Next, large rollers squeeze the corn flat into flakes. After that, the corn flakes are toasted in ovens.

The corn flakes are put into bags and then boxes.

Trucks take the boxes to stores.

44

PRACTICE

- Ask students to turn to **Student WorkText, page 45.**
  Have them preview the article and complete the *Before
  You Read* prompt. (See **Preview Routine, page 20.**)

- Ask students to read the article silently, paying special
  attention to the flow chart. Then have students answer the
  As You Read questions on their own.

 Have students model aloud how they read the
flow chart. Use the following prompts, as needed.

  ✔ What part of the flow chart did you read first?

  ✔ How did you know the order of the steps?

  ✔ How did the flow chart fit in with the article?

- Discuss the article and flow chart using the *After You Read* questions as
  a starting point. You may also wish to ask: *Is a flow chart like a time
  line in any way? Explain. Why did the author include a flow chart in the
  article?*

- Have volunteers share their pair-share discussion with the class.

Retelling   Model retelling of the text. Involve students by having them
add one or two of the details.

APPLY

- Ask students to turn to **Student WorkText, page 46.**
  Before students begin making their flow charts, suggest
  that they first visualize the steps in making the sandwich
  of their choice, write them on scrap paper, and then
  check to be sure the order is correct.

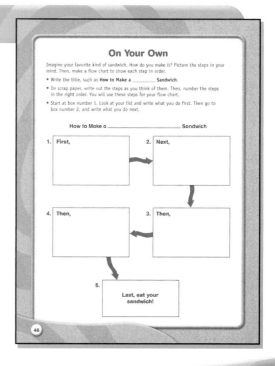

LESSON **14** Flow Charts

TEACH

- Ask students to turn to **Student WorkText, page 47**.

- Have students read the page silently before discussing together the flow chart and steps for reading it.

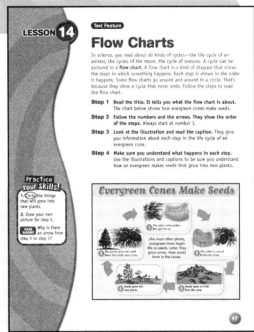

TEACHER THINK ALOUD This flow chart is very much like the one in "A Farmer's Year," so you probably have a good idea of how to read it. Let me quickly show you how I read it.

As always, I read the title first to find out what the flow chart shows. This flow chart shows how evergreens grow.

Once again, I see numbers and arrows. I start at number 1, look at the illustration carefully to see what information it gives, and read the caption. If there's something I don't understand, I reread. If I'm still stuck, I put a sticky note on what I don't understand and talk to someone about it later.

I continue in this way, following the arrows and numbers in order until I come to the last step in the flow chart.

- Have students follow the directions and answer the questions under *Practice Your Skills*. Check their answers and assist them, as needed, in interpreting the flow chart.

- Ask students to turn to **Student WorkText, page 48.** Have them preview the article and complete the *Before You Read* prompt. (See **Preview Routine, page 20.**)

- Ask students to read the article silently, paying special attention to the flow chart. Tell them to answer the *As You Read* questions on their own.

 Have students model aloud how they read the flow chart. Use the following prompts, as needed:

✔ What did you look at first? Why?

✔ Why is it important to follow the steps in order?

✔ How does the flow chart relate to the article?

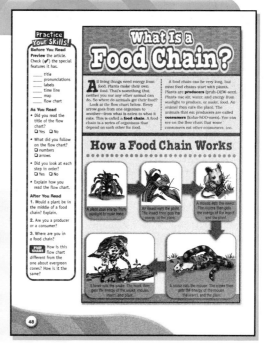

- Discuss the article and flow chart using the *After You Read* questions as a starting point. You may also wish to ask: *Did you get stuck anywhere in the reading? What did you do?* and *What's one thing we all have had for breakfast at some time, like bread or cereal with milk? Let's make up a food chain for one of the foods.*

Retelling Model retelling the text. Involve students by having them add one or two of the details. If needed, demonstrate "look backs" by rereading aloud particular parts of the article to refresh students' memories.

APPLY

- Ask students to turn to **Student WorkText, page 49.**

- Have students read the directions and follow the steps to make a flow chart.

- Discuss students' answers to the questions in *You Be the Expert!*

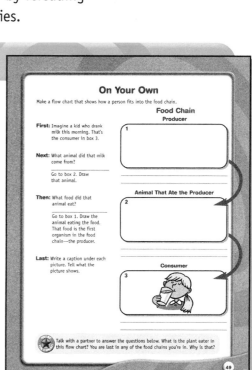

LESSON 15 Sequence

TEACH

Text Structure: Sequence

- Remind students that writers of nonfiction often organize their writing in one of five ways: description, sequence, compare/contrast, cause/effect, or problem/solution. Knowing how the writing is organized helps readers understand and remember what they read. Display the **Text Structures Poster**. (See **Student WorkText, page 105**.)

- The text structure of "From Peanuts to Peanut Butter" is sequence. You may wish to use the *Think Aloud* as you model how to determine the sequence text structure of the article.

> **TEACHER THINK ALOUD** I know that writers organize their writing in a way that helps us better understand and remember the information. So I'd like to go over what I did to figure out how this article is organized. The title makes me think the writer is going to explain the steps that happen to make peanuts into peanut butter. The headings show a sequence too.
>
> As I read, I see the words *in April, fall, first, next, then, after that,* and *finally*. These words are clues that the writer is telling me about a sequence. So I'll pay attention to what happens first, next, and after that to the peanuts on the farm.
>
> The flow chart will help me understand how the harvested peanuts become peanut butter because it shows the steps in order.

Build Background: Smart Chart

- Use the **Smart Chart Routine, page 19**. Through your questioning, guide the discussion to identify students' knowledge and/or misconceptions about how peanuts are grown and peanut butter is made.

Preteach Vocabulary

- Define each of the words below from "From Peanuts to Peanut Butter." Provide a context sentence and point out multiple meanings. (See **Vocabulary Routine, page 21.**)

harvest   To gather and bring in crops. *Fall is the time to **harvest** many crops.*

factory   A building or plant where something is made. *Thousands of crayons are made daily at the **factory**.*

ground 1. Crushed into small pieces. *The nuts were **ground** into tiny pieces.* **2.** Soil, dirt, earth. *The **ground** was too hard to plant seeds.*

consumer   A person who buys something. *Many **consumers** flocked to the store for the sale.*

- Ask students to turn to **Student WorkText, pages 50–51**. Direct their attention to *Before You Read*. Have them fill in the vocabulary chart.

Word	Synonym
crushed	*ground*
gather	*harvest*
soil	*ground*
buyer	*consumer*
plant	*factory*

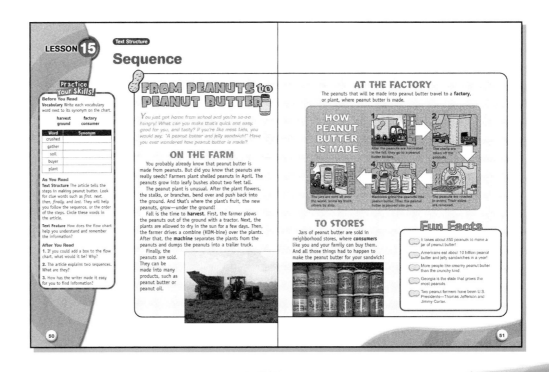

Read the Article

● Read aloud the *As You Read* text to help students set a purpose for reading. Then, ask students to read the article silently, paying special attention to the flow chart.

● When students have finished reading, discuss the article and flow chart using the *After You Read* questions.

Check Comprehension

● Have students retell the selection in their own words. Encourage them to include as many details from the article as they can recall. (See pages 21–23 for a detailed discussion of retellings.)

● You may wish to continue the discussion with these and other questions:

✔ What is unusual about the peanut plant?

✔ What are some other foods that go through many stages as they are made in a factory?

✔ Why did the author include a definition of "stalks" in the second paragraph?

✔ What features did the author include to make the information clear? **NAEP**

Graphic Organizer

● Ask students to turn to **Student WorkText, page 52.**

● Have them reread the article to determine any information left out of their retellings. Then ask students to complete the graphic organizer to show what happens on the farm.

● When finished, have students do a second retelling to a partner.

● Use a graphic organizer such as this when students encounter this text structure in their social studies and science textbooks.

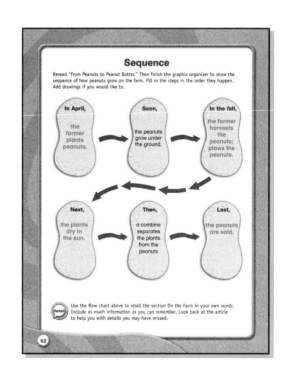

APPLY

Writing Frame

- Ask students to turn to **Student WorkText, page 53**.

- Remind students that writers use certain words and phrases when writing about a sequence. These words include *first, next, then, after that, last,* and *finally*. These words and phrases are called *signal words*. They help readers organize their thinking about the text.

- Have students complete the sequence writing frame using the information in the article on pages 50–51. Work with students, as needed.

On Your Own

- Have students write their own sequence paragraph using information from their social studies textbook. Students may write about how a particular crop is grown, such as wheat or corn, or how a food is made, such as pasta, pretzels, or grape jam.

- Explain to students that the more practice they have using the sequence writing frame, the more familiar they will be with this text structure. This will help them recognize the sequence pattern as they read, inform them about how to organize their thinking about their reading, and improve their reading comprehension overall. These writing frames can also be used when they answer test questions or write reports for social studies and science assignments.

Writing Frame

Use the information in your graphic organizer to fill in the writing frame.

This is how peanuts grow. In April, _the farmer plants peanuts_

Then, in the fall, _the farmer harvests the peanuts;_ plows up the peanuts

Next, the plants have to _dry in the sun_

After that, _a combine separates the plants from the peanuts_

and _puts the peanuts into a truck_

Last, the peanuts are sold.

Use the writing frame above as a model to write about another sequence, such as how corn or wheat is grown. Or how a food such as pasta is made. Look in your social studies textbook if you need facts that will help you fill in the frame.

53

LESSON 16 Headings

Textbook articles are organized to help readers understand important information.

- The title often states the topic—who or what the article is about.

- The introduction often states the main idea, the most important idea, of the entire article.

- **Headings** give information about the main idea of each part of an article. Headings often have some special type treatment. They may be boldfaced, all capital letters, or shown in a color other than black.

- Details give information about or describe the main idea. Under each heading are facts, examples, or descriptions, that add information about the main idea.

- A preview of the title, introduction, and headings informs readers of the topic and main ideas in the text and prepares them for the information that follows.

TEACH

- Ask students to turn to **Student WorkText, page 54.**

- Have students read the page silently before discussing together the article and steps to read it.

TEACHER THINK ALOUD Previewing an article gets you ready for what you're going to read. Let me show you how. First, I read the title. The title tells me that this article is about animal babies, specifically the babies of endangered animals. Next I study the headings. They tell me the names of the animals. Then I read the introduction, which tells me where they live—a zoo. Then, I look for special type, such as boldfaced words to identify important words in the article. Using all this information, I ask myself, "What will this article be about?" Now I know what the important ideas are and I am ready to read the article.

- Have students follow the directions and answer the question under *Practice Your Skills*. Check their answers and assist them, as needed, in using the headings to determine main ideas.

PRACTICE

- Ask students to turn to **Student WorkText, page 55.** Have them preview the article and complete the *Before You Read* prompt. (See **Preview Routine, page 20.**)

- Ask students to read the article silently, paying special attention to the headings. Then tell them to answer the *As You Read* questions on their own.

 Have students model aloud how they read the article. Use the following prompts, as needed:

✔ What did you look at first?

✔ How did the headings get you ready to read?

✔ What are the main ideas in the article? Where did you find them?

- Discuss the article using the *After You Read* questions. You may also wish to ask: *How do elephants communicate? Why are scientists studying elephant communication?*

Retelling   Model retelling the text. Involve students by having them add one or two of the details. If needed, demonstrate "look backs" by rereading aloud particular parts of the article to refresh students' memories.

APPLY

- Ask students to turn to **Student WorkText, page 56.**

- Have students mark up the article as prompted.

- Use the *You Be the Expert!* questions to spark discussion about the text and help students interpret the information it contains. Have students answer each other's questions.

- You may wish to continue the discussion with these and other questions:

✔ How many different ways to communicate did you learn about in the article? Tell about each one.

✔ What ways have you seen or heard animals use to communicate? What do you think the animals were trying to say?

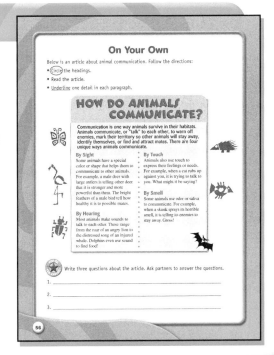

LESSON 17 Headings

CONNECTING TO YOUR CURRICULUM

Headings

Most of the articles in your social studies and science textbooks will be organized using headings and subheadings. Use these as opportunities to reinforce students' skills.

Social Studies

- Use any section of your textbook that contains clear main idea headings and subheadings. This skill applies to most text students will encounter in their social studies textbooks

Science

- Use any section of your textbook that contains clear main idea headings and subheadings. This skill applies to most text students will encounter in their science textbooks.

TEACH

- Ask students to turn to **Student WorkText, page 57**.

- Have students read the page silently before discussing together the sample article and steps to read it.

TEACHER THINK ALOUD First, I read the title of the article. It tells me that this article will be about why communities change over time. Next, I read the headings. They list three ways in which communities change over time. These are the main ideas in the article. Finally, I read the article to learn more facts or details about communities and how they change.

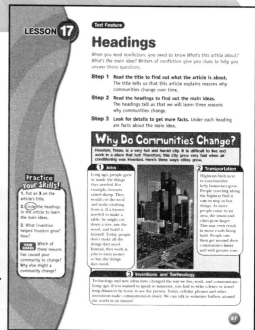

- Have students follow the directions and answer the questions under *Practice Your Skills*. Check their answers and assist them, as needed, in using the headings.

PRACTICE

- Ask students to turn to **Student WorkText, page 58.**
  Have them preview the article and complete the *Before You Read* prompt.

- Ask students to read the article silently, paying special attention to the features that help them determine the main ideas and details in the article. Tell them to answer the *As You Read* questions on their own.

Have students model aloud how they read the article. Use the following prompts, as needed:

- ✔ What did you look at first?
- ✔ What did the headings tell you about rivers?
- ✔ How were the pictures helpful?

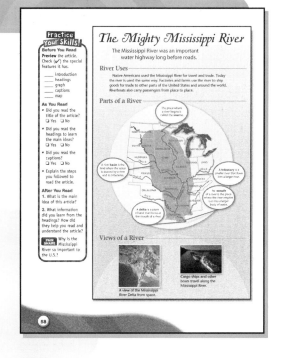

- Discuss the article using the *After You Read* questions. Have volunteers share their pair-share discussions with the class.

Retelling Model retelling the text. Involve students by having them add one or two of the details. If needed, demonstrate "look backs" by rereading aloud particular parts of the article to refresh students' memories. *I am going to retell the selection, but I'm going to leave out one or two important details. Listen closely and tell me what else I should add.*

APPLY

- Ask students to turn to **Student WorkText, page 59.**

- Have students complete the outline describing the topic, main ideas, and details of the text. Discuss the format of the article and how it helped students understand it. Ask: *What other text features could be added to this article?*

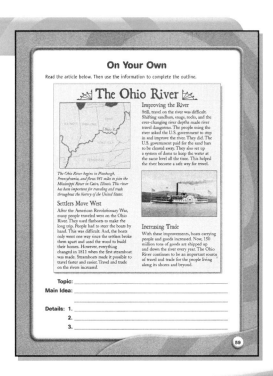

LESSON 18 · Sequence

TEACH

Text Structure: Sequence

- Discuss the importance of identifying how a text is structured. Tell students that figuring out how a selection is structured will help them organize their thinking as they read. Explain that a writer often uses signal words as clues to what the text structure is. Display the **Text Structures Poster**. (See **Student WorkText, page 105**.)

> **TEACHER THINK ALOUD** I know that writers organize their writing in a way that helps us better understand and remember the information. In the article "Sea Turtles on the Move," the writer has a special section detailing the steps a female turtle takes to find a place to lay her eggs. As I read, I will look for this sequence of events. I'll look for clue words that help me. Words such as *first, next, after that*, and *finally* are clues that the author is describing the order in which the events take place.

Build Background: Smart Chart

- Use the **Smart Chart Routine, page 19**. Through your questioning, guide the discussion to identify students' knowledge and/or misconceptions about animal migration.

Preteach Vocabulary

- Define each of the following words from "Sea Turtles on the Move." Provide a context sentence and point out any related words. (See **Vocabulary Routine, page 21.**)

migrate   To move from one place to another. *Many birds migrate south every winter.*
Related words: *migration, immigrant, immigration, migratory, migrant*

odor   A smell. *I love the odor of fresh apples.*
Related word: *smell*

marine   To do with the sea. *A whale is a marine animal.*
Related words: *marina, maritime, Marines*

creature   A living being, such as a person or animal. *That sea creature had eight legs.* Useful word part: *-ture*

- Ask students to turn to **Student WorkText, pages 60–61**. Direct their attention to *Before You Read* and have them complete the questions before they begin to read the article.

Read the Article

- Read aloud the *As You Read* text to help students set a purpose for reading. Then, ask students to read the article silently, paying special attention to the headings.

- When students have finished reading, discuss the article using the *After You Read* questions.

Check Comprehension

- Have students retell the section called "Returning to a Place to Lay Her Eggs" in their own words. Encourage them to include as many details from the article as they can recall and use sequence words in their retelling.

- You may wish to continue the discussion with these and other questions:
  - ✔ Why do sea turtles migrate?
  - ✔ How do scientists know that turtles use their noses to migrate?
  - ✔ What is a hatchling?
  - ✔ What dangers do sea turtles face? Why?

Graphic Organizer

- Ask students to turn to **Student WorkText, page 62.**

- Have them reread the article to determine any information left out of their retellings. Then ask students to complete the graphic organizer to highlight details about the steps a sea turtle takes to lay its eggs.

- When finished, have students do a second retelling to a partner.

- Use a graphic organizer such as this whenever students encounter sequence paragraphs in their social studies and science textbooks.

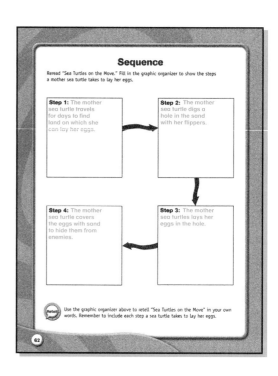

APPLY

Writing Frame

- Ask students to turn to **Student WorkText, page 63**.

- Remind students that writers use certain words and phrases when writing sequence paragraphs. These include *first, then, next, after that,* and *finally*. These words and phrases are called *signal words*. They signal that the author is providing information about the time order of events. This helps readers organize their thinking about the text.

- Have students complete the sequence writing frame using the information in the article on pages 60–61. Work with students, as needed.

On Your Own

- Have students write their own sequence paragraph using the sequence writing frame and information from their social studies textbook. Students will write about the life cycle of another animal.

- Explain to students that the more practice they have using the sequence writing frame, the more familiar they will be with this text structure. This will assist them in recognizing the sequence pattern as they read, inform them as to how to organize their thinking about their reading and writing, and improve their reading comprehension overall.

LESSON 19 Graphs

A **graph** is a drawing used to represent numerical information quickly and easily. It is possible to quickly make comparisons that would otherwise take several sentences, and even paragraphs, to present.

A **pictograph**, or picture graph, uses simple pictures to represent numerical information.

- A pictograph includes a **key** that tells the amount each symbol represents.

- It may be necessary to multiply the number of **symbols** by the amount each symbol represents.

A **bar graph** uses vertical or horizontal **bars** to show comparative amounts.

- The length of the bar is determined by the quantity being represented.

- A bar graph includes a title, labels along one axis, and numbers along the other.

TEACH

- Ask students to turn to **Student WorkText, page 64**.

- Have students read the page silently before discussing together the sample pictograph and steps to read it.

TEACHER THINK ALOUD This graph is called a pictograph. You can see that it uses small pictures, or symbols, instead of a solid bar. Each symbol represents an amount, or a number.

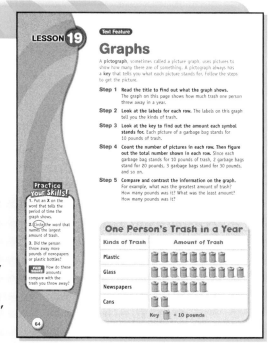

Let's follow the steps to learn how to read a pictograph. We begin by looking at the title: "One Person's Trash in a Year." This tells us what the pictograph will be about. In this graph, we will learn about the amount of trash a person throws out in a year.

Then we look at the labels on a pictograph. They are on the left-hand side. Put your finger on them. The labels name types of trash. There are no numbers to show amounts. Instead, there are symbols. How do we know what they stand for? We have to look at the graph's key. It tells us that each symbol stands for 10 pounds.

Next, we trace each line with our finger to find the amount of trash thrown out in one year. Put your finger on the word *Cans*. Then count the number of symbols. There are two symbols, so that equals 20 pounds of trash. Continue doing this for the other types of trash.

When you're done, think about which type of trash was thrown out the most, the least, and how one type of trash compares to another.

- Have students follow the directions and answer the questions under *Practice Your Skills*. Check their answers and assist them, as needed, in interpreting the graph.

- Ask students to turn to **Student WorkText, page 65.** Have them preview the article and complete the *Before You Read* prompt. (See **Preview Routine, page 20.**)

- Ask students to read the article silently, paying special attention to the pictograph. Tell them to answer the *As You Read* questions on their own.

STUDENT THINK ALOUD Have students model how they read the graph. Use the following prompts, as needed:

✔ What did you look at first?

✔ How did you know what each drop of water stood for?

✔ How did you figure out which activity used the most water? the least?

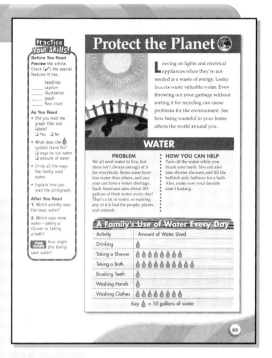

- Discuss the article and graph using the *After You Read* questions. You may also wish to ask: *Why did the author put the information on a graph instead of just writing it in words within the article?* **NAEP**

Retelling   Model retelling the text. Demonstrate "look backs" by rereading aloud particular parts of the article to refresh students' memories. *I am going to retell the selection, but I'm going to leave out one or two important details. Listen closely and tell me what I should add.*

APPLY

- Ask students to turn to **Student WorkText, page 66.**

- Have students study the graph in order to write three questions about its content. Before they begin, orally brainstorm with students sample questions using the words and phrases in the word list.

- Ask students to trade papers with a partner and answer each other's questions. Then provide time for students to share their questions and answers with the class.

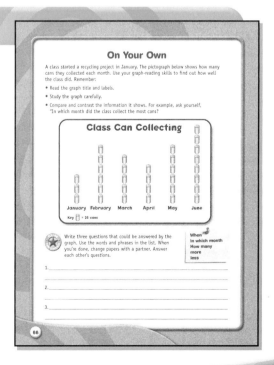

TEACH

• Ask students to turn to **Student WorkText, page 67**.

• Have students read the page silently before discussing together the sample bar graph and steps to read it.

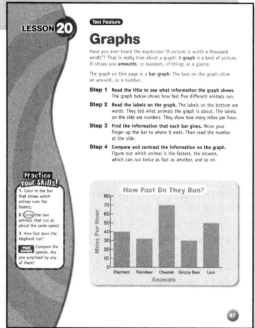

TEACHER THINK ALOUD This graph looks very different from the pictographs we've been reading. It is called a bar graph. Each bar shows an amount, or a number. Let's follow the steps to learn how to read a bar graph.

First, we look at the title: "How Fast Do They Run?" This tells us what the bar graph will be about. In this graph, we will learn about animal speeds.

Then we look at the labels. Put your finger on the labels at the bottom. They name animals. Now, put your finger at the labels on the left-hand side. They are numbers that tell us speeds in miles per hour.

Next, we trace each bar with a finger to find the speed each animal can run. Let's try one together. Put your finger on the word *elephant*. Now trace the bar upward. Where it stops, run your finger to the left to find the amount. That's right, it's 40 miles per hour. Continue doing this for the other animals.

Finally, let's think about the information on the graph: Which animal runs the fastest? the slowest? How does one animal's speed compare to another? Were there any surprises?

• Have students follow the directions and answer the questions under *Practice Your Skills*. Check their answers and assist them, as needed, in interpreting the graph.

PRACTICE

- Ask students to turn to **Student WorkText, page 68**. Have them preview the article and complete the *Before You Read* prompt. (See **Preview Routine, page 20**.)

- Ask students to read the article silently, paying special attention to the bar graph. Tell them to answer the *As You Read* questions on their own.

STUDENT THINK ALOUD Have students model aloud how they read the graph. Use the following prompts, as needed:

✔ What did you look at first?

✔ How did you know the speed of each ball? Show what you did with your finger to figure out the speeds.

✔ How did you figure out which ball was the fastest? the slowest?

- Discuss the article and graph using the *After You Read* questions. You may also wish to ask: *Were you surprised by any of the speeds? How fast is a tennis serve? How would slowing down the ball help make tennis more interesting? What sports on the list do you play?*

Retelling Model retelling of the text. Involve students by having them add one or two of the details.

APPLY

- Ask students to turn to **Student WorkText, page 69**.

- Have students use The Facts paragraph to create a bar graph. Assist them, as needed.

- Use the *You Be the Expert!* question to spark discussion about the graph and help students interpret the information it contains.

- You may wish to continue the discussion with these and other questions:

✔ Which animal in the graph has the shortest life span?

✔ How did you mark the age 45 on the chart? Why?

✔ How is information in a paragraph different from information in a graph? Which is easier for you to read? **NAEP**

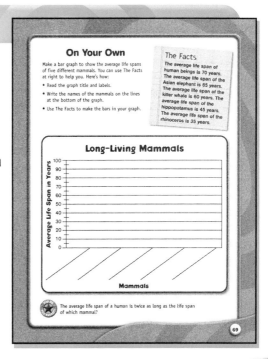

TEACH

Text Structure: Compare/Contrast

- Discuss the importance of identifying how a text is structured. Explain that a writer often uses signal words as clues to what the text structure is. Display the **Text Structures Poster**. (See **Student WorkText, page 105.**)

> **TEACHER THINK ALOUD** I know that writers organize their writing in a way that helps us better understand and remember the information. In the article "What Is Congress?" the writer compares and contrasts the two groups that make up the U.S. Congress—the Senate and the House of Representatives. As I read, I will look for how the Senate and the House are the same and how they are different. I'll look for clue words that help me. Words such as *both, also*, and *too* are clues that things are alike. Words such as *however* and *but* are clues that they are different.

Build Background: Smart Chart

- Use the **Smart Chart Routine, page 19**. Through your questioning, guide the discussion to identify students' knowledge and/or misconceptions about Congress.

Preteach Vocabulary

- Define each of the following words from "What Is Congress?" Provide a context sentence and point out any related words. (See **Vocabulary Routine, page 21.**)

elect   To choose for office by voting. *We elect a president every four years.*
Related word: *election*

Congress   The branch of U.S. government that makes our laws. *Congress is made up of the Senate and the House of Representatives.*

senator   A member of the U.S. Senate; serves a six-year term. *The Senate has 100 members, two senators from each state.*

representative   A member of the U.S. House of Representatives; serves a two-year term. *There are presently 435 representatives.*

Ask students to turn to **Student WorkText, pages 70–71.** Direct their attention to *Before You Read* and have them complete the Knowledge Chart before they begin to read the article.

KNOWLEDGE CHART

What We Do	Who They Are	What They Do
elect	Congress senators representatives	make laws

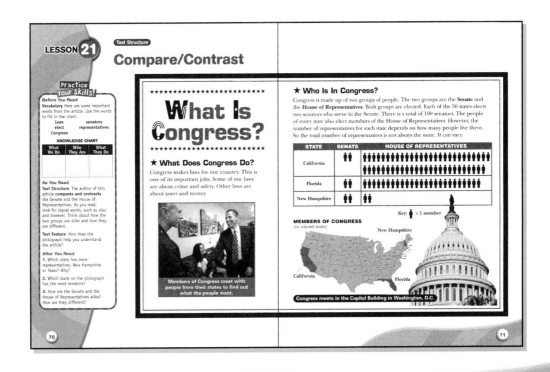

Read the Article

- Read aloud the *As You Read* text to help students set a purpose for reading. Then, ask students to read the article silently, paying special attention to the pictograph on page 71.

- When students have finished reading, discuss the article and graph using the *After You Read* questions.

Check Comprehension

- Have students retell the selection in their own words. Encourage them to include as many details from the article as they can recall. (See pages 21–23 for a detailed discussion of retellings.)

- You may wish to continue the discussion with these and other questions:
  - ✔ Where does Congress meet? Why?
  - ✔ How many senators does California have? Florida? How many representatives do these two states have?
  - ✔ Why are the number of representatives different from state to state? Do you think this is a fair system? Why or why not?
  - ✔ How is the federal government like your state government?

Graphic Organizer

- Ask students to turn to **Student WorkText, page 72.**

- Have them reread the article and complete the graphic organizer.

- When finished, have students do a second retelling to a partner.

- Use a graphic organizer such as a Venn diagram whenever students encounter compare/contrast paragraphs in their social studies and science textbooks.

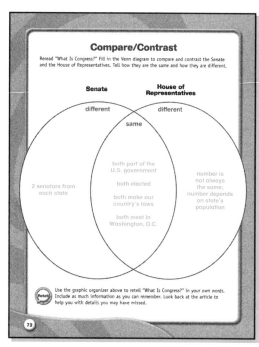

APPLY

Writing Frame

- Ask students to turn to **Student WorkText, page 73**.

- Remind students that writers use certain words and phrases when writing compare/contrast paragraphs. These include *both, same, different, so, therefore, but, unlike, however,* and *in contrast to*. These words and phrases are called *signal words*. They signal that the writer is comparing or contrasting information.

- Have students complete the compare/contrast writing frame using the information in the article on pages 70–71. Work with students, as needed.

On Your Own

- Have students write their own compare/contrast paragraph using the compare/contrast writing frame and information from their social studies textbook. Students will compare and contrast the jobs of mayor and governor.

- Explain to students that the more practice they have using the compare/contrast writing frame, the more familiar they will be with this text structure. This will assist them in recognizing the compare/contrast pattern as they read, inform them about how to organize their thinking about their reading and writing, and improve their reading comprehension overall.

LESSON 22 Time Lines

TEACH

- Ask students to turn to **Student WorkText, page 74.**

- Have students read the page silently before discussing together the sample time line and steps for reading it.

TEACHER THINK ALOUD I'd like to show you how I read this time line. I begin with the title to find out what the time line is about. This time line shows when certain things happened in the White House for the very first time. What do I look at next? I read the first date and the last date. That shows me how much time is covered. This time line goes from 1800 to 2000. That's 200 years.

I know there must have been a lot that happened in 200 years! To find out, I read the first date, 1800. Then I follow the line to the caption because I want to know what happened that year. I learn that the White House was finished being built. That means the White House was 200 years old in the year 2000!

To find out what happened after that, I read each date and caption in order. The next thing I learn is that the White House got running water in 1833. I wonder how they got water to wash clothes and dishes and themselves before then? There's a lot of interesting information on this time line!

- Have students follow the directions and answer the questions under *Practice Your Skills*. Check their answers and assist them, as needed, in interpreting the time line.

PRACTICE

- Ask students to turn to **Student WorkText, page 75.** Direct students to *Before You Read.* Have them preview the article and respond. (See **Preview Routine, page 20.**)

- Ask students to read the article silently, paying special attention to the time line. Then have students answer the *As You Read* questions on their own.

 Have students model aloud how they read the time line. Use the following prompts, as needed:

✔ What did you read first?

✔ How did you figure out how much time is covered?

✔ Why is it important to read the dates and events in order?

- Discuss the article and time line using the *After You Read* questions as a starting point. You may also wish to ask: *How does the information in the time line help you understand what you read in the article?*

Retelling Model retelling of the text. If needed, demonstrate "look backs" by rereading aloud parts of the article to refresh students' memories. *I am going to retell the selection, but I'm going to leave out one or two important details. Listen closely and tell me what else I should add.*

APPLY

- Ask students to turn to **Student WorkText, page 76.** Have them read The Facts and make a time line based on the information. Discuss: *How could your time line help someone who is reading about Benjamin Franklin?*

- You may wish to continue the discussion with these and other questions:

✔ What other topics could you make a time line about?

✔ How does a time line about Benjamin Franklin compare with a book about Franklin? What would you learn from each one?

✔ How is a time line different from other diagrams you've seen?

LESSON 23 Time Lines

CONNECTING TO YOUR CURRICULUM

Time Lines

You will find these and other time lines in your social studies and science textbooks. Use these as opportunities to reinforce students' skills.

Social Studies

- Westward expansion
- lives of important Americans
- major events in American history
- history of a community

Science

- history of flight
- exploration of space
- lives of famous scientists
- discoveries and inventions

TEACH

- Ask students to turn to **Student WorkText, page 77**.

- Have students read the page silently before discussing together the sample time line and steps for reading it.

TEACHER THINK ALOUD Let's follow the steps together to read the time line on this page. First, we look at the title to find out what the time line is about. This time line is about the history of sports and games.

The first date is 1611, and the last date is 2000. This tells us that the time line will show information about sports between 1611 and 2000. How many years is that? Right, 389 years.

Notice that the dates go in order, from the earliest to the latest. Also, you can see that not every single year between 1611 and 2000 is included. That's because time lines show only the years when some important event related to the topic happened.

- Have students follow the directions and answer the questions under *Practice Your Skills*. Check their answers and assist them, as needed, in interpreting the time line.

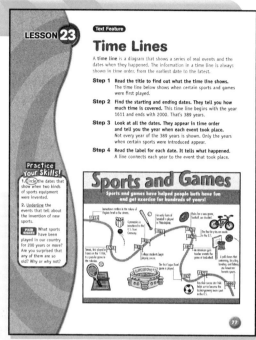

PRACTICE

- Ask students to turn to **Student WorkText, page 78.** Direct students to *Before You Read*. Have them preview the article and respond. (See **Preview Routine, page 20.**)

- Ask students to read the article silently, paying special attention to the time line. Tell them to answer the *As You Read* questions on their own.

Have students model aloud how they read the time line. Use the following prompts, as needed:

- ✔ What did you look at first? Why?

- ✔ How did you figure out how many years the time line covers?

- ✔ How did you read the time line?

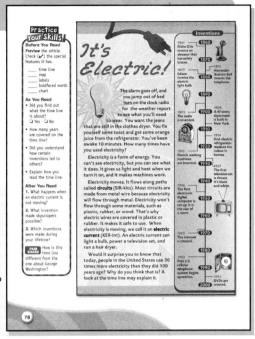

- Discuss the article and time line using the *After You Read* questions as a starting point. Ask: *Why do people today use more electricity than people 100 years ago? Look on the time line. What invention made very tall buildings possible? Which inventions are the most important in your life? Why do you think the writer included the time line?*

- Have volunteers share their pair-share discussion with the class.

Retelling Model retelling the text. Involve students by having them add one or two of the details.

APPLY

- Ask students to turn to **Student WorkText, page 79.**

- Have students read the directions and follow the steps to make a time line about themselves. You may wish to discuss: *How will you decide on the beginning and end dates? How will you decide which other dates and information to include on your time line?* Suggest to students that they use another sheet of paper to write their dates and events as they think of them. Then they can transfer the information to their time line in the correct time order.

- Ask students to read the directions in *You Be The Expert!* Before they begin writing questions, orally brainstorm sample questions that use the words in the word list.

- Have students trade papers with a partner and answer each other's questions.

TEACH

Text Structure: Problem/Solution

- Remind students that writers of nonfiction often organize their writing in one of five ways: description, sequence, compare/contrast, cause/effect, or problem/solution. Knowing how the writing is organized helps readers understand and remember what they read. Display the **Text Structures Poster**. (See **Student WorkText, page 105**.)

- The text structure of "A Son Remembers" is problem/solution. You may wish to use the *Think Aloud* as you model how to determine the problem/solution text structure of the article.

TEACHER THINK ALOUD I know that writers organize their writing in a way that helps us better understand and remember the information, so as I read I try to figure out how this article is organized.

The writer tells us in the first paragraph that the King family was not free to do what they enjoyed. This tells me that there were problems facing the family. As I continue reading, I look for what those problems were.

Then the writer says that Dr. Martin Luther King, Jr., led protest marches and gave speeches in favor of equality for African Americans. In other words, he took steps to solve the problems. The writer also includes the words *because* of and *as a result* signals that we are going to learn what those solutions were. Since I know what the text structure of the article is, I look for the problems and solutions as I read.

Build Background: Smart Chart

- Use the **Smart Chart Routine, page 19**. Through your questioning, guide the discussion to identify students' knowledge and/or misconceptions about Dr. Martin Luther King, Jr., and his son, Martin Luther King III.

Preteach Vocabulary

- Define each of the following words from "A Son Remembers." Provide a context sentence and point out related words. (See **Vocabulary Routine, page 21**.)

civil rights   People's rights under the law. *The U.S. Constitution guarantees civil rights for all Americans, regardless of race or religion.*

equality   The same rights for everyone. *Dr. King led a peaceful fight for equality, no matter how we look or what our beliefs are.*
Related word: *equal*

prejudice   Negative judgment of someone based on a person's race or religion. *Martin Luther King III continues to fight prejudice against any group.*

segregated   Separated or kept apart. *Separate schools for white children and African-American children kept the groups segregated for many years.*
Related word: *segregation*

● Ask students to turn to **Student WorkText, pages 80–81**. Direct their attention to *Before You Read* and have them complete the chart before they begin to read the article.

Dr. King was against	Dr. King worked for
segregation	*civil rights*
prejudice	*equality*

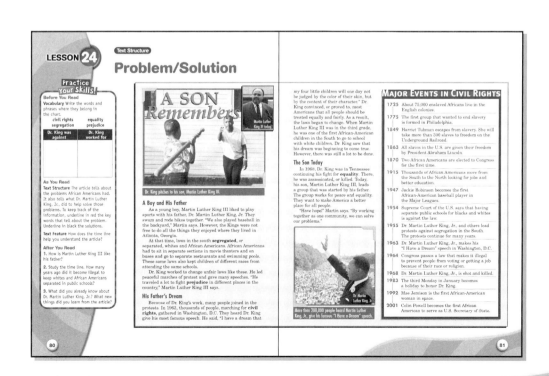

Read the Article

● Read aloud the *As You Read* text to help students set a purpose for reading. Then, ask students to read the article silently, paying special attention to the time line.

● When students have finished reading, discuss the article and time line using the *After You Read* questions.

Check Comprehension

● Have students retell the selection in their own words. Encourage them to include as many details from the article as they can recall. (See pages 21–23 for a detailed discussion of retellings.)

● You may wish to continue the discussion with these and other questions:

✔ How is Martin Luther King III like his father?

✔ What event happened in the years between Dr. King's famous speech and his death?

✔ Use the context in the article to tell the meaning of *convinced*.

✔ What did the author do to present the information clearly? **NAEP**

Graphic Organizer

● Ask students to turn to **Student WorkText, page 82.**

● Have them reread the article to determine any information left out of their retellings. Then ask students to complete the graphic organizer. Tell students that they should include information from the time line to fill in the What Finally Happened box.

● When finished, have students do a second retelling to a partner.

● Use a graphic organizer such as this when students encounter this text structure in their social studies and science textbooks.

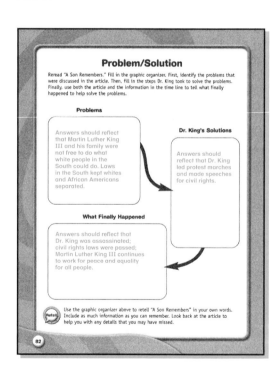

Problem/Solution

Reread "A Son Remembers." Fill in the graphic organizer. First, identify the problems that were discussed in the article. Then, fill in the steps Dr. King took to solve the problems. Finally, use both the article and the information in the time line to tell what finally happened to help solve the problems.

Problems

Answers should reflect that Martin Luther King III and his family were not free to do what white people in the South could do. Laws in the South kept whites and African Americans separated.

Dr. King's Solutions

Answers should reflect that Dr. King led protest marches and made speeches for civil rights.

What Finally Happened

Answers should reflect that Dr. King was assassinated; civil rights laws were passed; Martin Luther King III continues to work for peace and equality for all people.

Use the graphic organizer above to retell "A Son Remembers" in your own words. Include as much information as you can remember. Look back at the article to help you with any details that you may have missed.

82

APPLY

Writing Frame

- Ask students to turn to **Student WorkText, page 83**.

- Have students complete the problem/solution writing frame using the information in the article on pages 80–81. Work with students, as needed.

On Your Own

- Have students write their own problem/solution paragraph about a problem in the environment, using information from their social studies textbook.

- Explain to students that the more practice they have using the problem/solution writing frame, the more familiar they will be with this text structure. This will help them recognize the problem/solution pattern as they read, inform them about how to organize their thinking about their reading, and improve their reading comprehension overall. These writing frames can also be used when they answer test questions or write reports for social studies and science assignments.

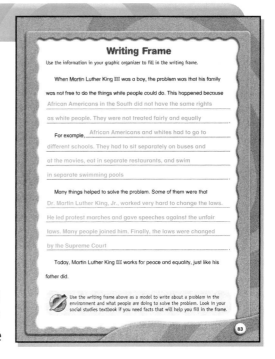

LESSON 25 Charts

A **chart** consists of information arranged in the form of a table. It provides a picture that helps readers "see the text." It makes complex material easier to understand and remember. For example, a chart of the number of calories in various popular foods can help readers decide which foods would be good for them to eat.

- The chart title identifies the chart topic.

- Column headings tell what kind of information will be found in each column. Column headings give readers a good idea of the main ideas that will be covered.

- Boldfaced words highlight the most important information in a chart. Other special treatment of type, such as capital letters, also highlight important information.

- Graphic aids, such as photographs and illustrations, make the chart more interesting and add information.

TEACH

- Ask students to turn to **Student WorkText, page 84**.

- Have students read the page silently before discussing together the sample chart and steps for reading it.

TEACHER THINK ALOUD Charts are a great way to see a lot of information in a limited space. Charts organize facts. Let's look at this chart. First, I read the title and introduction to find out what the chart is about. This chart shows some of the U.S. states that were named using Native American words. I know that Native American nations have lived in these areas for many hundreds of years, so the settlers must have kept the names already given to the areas.

Next, I read the headings in the chart. They tell me what information I will find in each column.

Finally, I read each row of text from left to right. For example, I see that the name *Alaska* comes from an Aleutian word. That is a language spoken by the people who have lived for centuries in what is now the state of Alaska. The name *Alaska* means "land that is not an island." This is a good name for Alaska, a large state with many smaller islands off its coast.

- Have students follow the directions and answer the questions under *Practice Your Skills*. Check their answers and assist them, as needed, in interpreting the chart.

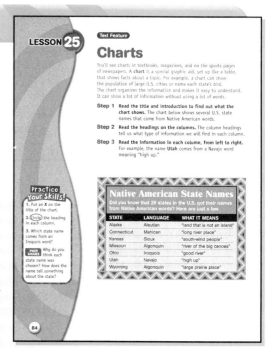

PRACTICE

- Ask students to turn to **Student WorkText, page 85.** Have them preview the article and complete the *Before You Read* prompt. (See **Preview Routine, page 20.**)

- Ask students to read the article silently, paying special attention to the chart. Then have students answer the *As You Read* questions on their own.

 THINK ALOUD Have students model aloud how they read the chart. Use the following prompts, as needed:

✔ What did you read first?

✔ How did you find out which animal is used for each year?

✔ How is this chart different from other charts you have seen?

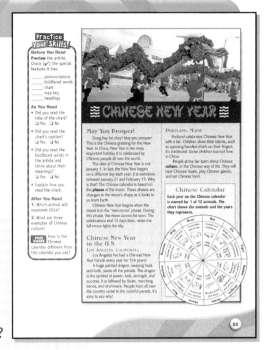

- Check students' answers. Then discuss the article and chart using the *After You Read* questions as a starting point. You may also wish to ask: *How does the information in the chart support the information in the article?*

- Have volunteers share their pair-share discussion with the class.

Retelling   Model retelling of the text. Involve students by having them add one or two of the details.

APPLY

- Ask students to turn to **Student WorkText, page 86.**

- Have students read the information about holidays.

- Then have them complete the chart.

- Discuss: *How could this chart help someone who is interested in learning about other cultures?*

- You may wish to spark discussion about the chart with these and other questions:

✔ Which holidays have you celebrated or seen celebrated during this time of year?

✔ Which holiday is celebrated in Mexico?

✔ Which holiday reminds you of Christmas? Why?

TEACH

- Ask students to turn to **Student WorkText, page 87**.
- Have students read the page silently before discussing together the sample chart and steps for reading it.

TEACHER THINK ALOUD   Let's look at this chart. First, I read the title to find out what the chart is about. The title "No Two Planets Are Alike" lets me know that the chart will detail ways in which the planets are different. Next, I read the column headings. They tell me that the chart will name a planet and give important facts about that planet's moons. Now I am ready to read the information in each row of the chart.

- Have students follow the directions and answer the question under *Practice Your Skills.* Check their answers and assist them, as needed, in noticing and using chart features.

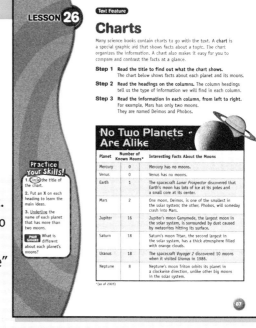

LESSON 26   Text Feature

Charts

Many science books contain charts to go with the text. A **chart** is a special graphic aid that shows facts about a topic. The chart organizes the information. A chart also makes it easy for you to compare and contrast the facts at a glance.

Step 1 Read the title to find out what the chart shows. The chart below shows facts about each planet and its moons.

Step 2 Read the headings on the columns. The column headings tell us the type of information we will find in each column.

Step 3 Read the information in each column, from left to right. For example, Mars has only two moons. They are named Deimos and Phobos.

Practice Your Skills!
1. Circle the title of the chart.
2. Put an **X** on each heading to learn the main ideas.
3. Underline the name of each planet that has more than two moons.

PAIR SHARE What is different about each planet's moons?

No Two Planets Are Alike

Planet	Number of Known Moons*	Interesting Facts About the Moons
Mercury	0	Mercury has no moons.
Venus	0	Venus has no moons.
Earth	1	The spacecraft *Lunar Prospector* discovered that Earth's moon has lots of ice at its poles and a small core at its center.
Mars	2	One moon, Deimos, is one of the smallest in the solar system; the other, Phobos, will someday crash into Mars.
Jupiter	16	Jupiter's moon Ganymede, the largest moon in the solar system, is surrounded by dust caused by meteorites hitting its surface.
Saturn	18	Saturn's moon Titan, the second largest in the solar system, has a thick atmosphere filled with orange clouds.
Uranus	18	The spacecraft *Voyager 2* discovered 10 moons when it visited Uranus in 1986.
Neptune	8	Neptune's moon Triton orbits its planet in a clockwise direction, unlike other big moons in the solar system.

*(as of 2005)

87

PRACTICE

- Ask students to turn to **Student WorkText, page 88.** Have students preview the article and complete the *Before You Read* prompt.

- Ask students to read the article silently, paying special attention to the chart. Then have students answer the *As You Read* questions on their own.

 STUDENT THINK ALOUD Have students model aloud how they read the chart. Use the following prompts, as needed:

- ✔ What do you read first?

- ✔ What is the purpose of the headings?

- ✔ What information does the chart provide?

- Discuss the article and text features using the *After You Read* questions as a starting point. You may also wish to ask: *How does the information in the chart support the information in the article?*

- Have volunteers share their pair-share discussion with the class.

Retelling Model retelling the text. If needed, demonstrate "look backs" by rereading aloud particular parts of the article to refresh students' memories. *I am going to retell the selection, but I'm going to leave out one or two important details. Listen closely and tell me what else I should add.*

APPLY

- Ask students to turn to **Student WorkText, page 89.**

- Have students complete the chart. Discuss: *How could this chart help someone learn more about Earth, Mars, and Jupiter?*

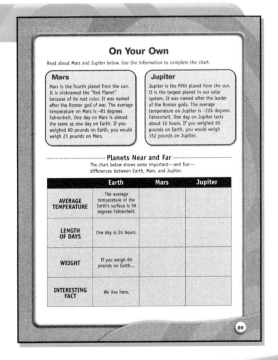

TEACH

Text Structure: Cause/Effect

- Discuss the importance of identifying how a text is structured. Tell students that figuring out how a selection is structured will help them organize their thinking as they read. Explain that writers often organize their writing to give clues to what the text structure is. Display the **Text Structures Poster**. (See **Student WorkText, page 105**.)

TEACHER THINK ALOUD I know that writers organize their writing in a way that helps us better understand and remember the information. In the article "Helping Earth's Animals" the writer tells the effects on animals of using too much water, wasting paper, or not keeping our beaches clean.

As I read, I will look for information about these effects. I will look for clue words that help me. For instance, words and phrases such as *because, as a result, cause,* and *in order to* are clues that the author is providing causes and effects of protecting the places in which animals live.

Build Background: Smart Chart

- Use the **Smart Chart Routine, page 19**. Through your questioning, guide the discussion to identify students' knowledge and/or misconceptions about recycling and conservation.

Preteach Vocabulary

- Define each of the following words from "Helping Earth's Animals."
  Provide a context sentence and point out any related words or useful
  word parts. (See **Vocabulary Routine, page 21.**)

  recycle   To process old items, such as glass, newspapers, and
  aluminum cans, so they can be used for new products.
  We recycle our newspapers at home.
  Point out the prefix *re-*, which means "again." Other words with this
  prefix include *remake, redo,* and *relive.*

  conserve   To save something from loss, damage, or decay.
  We turn out the lights when we leave the room to conserve energy.
  Related words include *conservation, conserved, conserving,* and
  conservative.

- Ask students to turn to **Student WorkText, pages 90–91.** Direct
  their attention to *Before You Read*. Then have students complete
  the sentence starters.

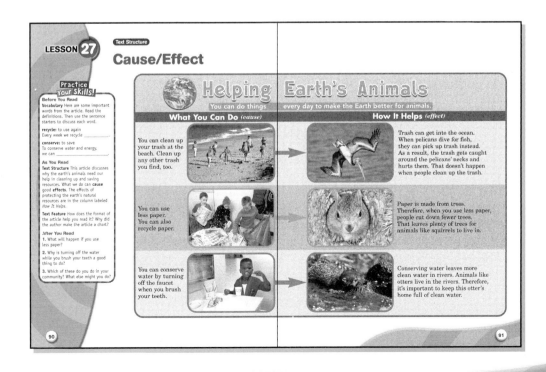

Read the Article

- Read aloud the *As You Read* text to help students set a purpose for reading. Then, ask students to read the article silently, paying special attention to the chart format.

- When students have finished reading, discuss the article and chart using the *After You Read* questions.

Check Comprehension

- Have students retell the selection in their own words. Encourage them to include as many details from the article as they can recall.

- You may wish to continue the discussion with these and other questions:

  ✔ Why is trash on the beach harmful to animals?

  ✔ How can using less paper help animals? Which animals can be helped?

  ✔ What is the difference between *recycling* and *conserving?*

  ✔ How does the format of an article change how you read it? **NAEP**

Graphic Organizer

- Ask students to turn to **Student WorkText, page 92.**

- Have them reread the article to determine any information left out of their retellings. Then ask students to complete the graphic organizer.

- When finished, have students do a second retelling to a partner.

- Use a graphic organizer such as this whenever students encounter cause/effect paragraphs in their social studies and science textbooks.

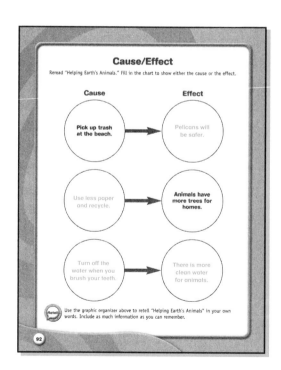

APPLY

Writing Frame

- Ask students to turn to **Student WorkText, page 93**.

- Remind students that writers use certain words and phrases when writing cause/effect paragraphs. These include *because, resulting from, therefore, consequently, due to, as a result,* and *effect*. These words and phrases are called *signal words*. They signal that the author is providing information about why something happened or what happened as a result of an event. This helps readers organize their thinking about the text.

- Have students complete the cause/effect writing frame using the information in the article on pages 90–91. Work with students, as needed.

On Your Own

- Have students write their own cause/effect paragraph using information from their science textbook. Students will write about the causes and effects of helping to recycle and conserve in their community.

- Explain to students that the more practice they have using the cause/effect writing frame, the more familiar they will be with this text structure. This will assist them in recognizing the cause/effect pattern as they read, inform them as to how to organize their thinking about their reading and writing, and improve their reading comprehension overall.

Writing Frame

Use the information in your graphic organizer to fill in the writing frame.

Many of Earth's animals are in danger. There are several things we can do to help them.

We can _____ clean up the trash at the beach _____

The effect of this is _____ it will protect sea animals, such as pelicans, who might be harmed or killed by the trash _____

We can also _____ use less paper and recycle what we do use _____

The effect of this is _____ forest animals will have more places to live and food to eat _____

In addition, we can _____ use less water when we bathe and brush our teeth _____. The effect of this is _____ there will be more river water for animals to drink and live in _____

Therefore, it's important to help Earth's animals so that they _____ will stay safe and alive _____

Use the writing frame above as a model to write a paragraph about helping your community. Begin like this, "We can do a lot to help our community." Look in your science textbook or local newspaper if you need facts that will help you.

93

LESSON 28 Maps

A **map** is a flat picture of part of Earth. There are five main types of maps: political, physical, landform, transportation, and historical.

- A political map shows information such as countries, states, and cities. These maps are used to show the borders between large, organized areas.

- A physical map shows Earth's natural features, such as mountains, oceans, and rivers. One type of physical map is the landform map.

- A landform map shows the shape of Earth's landmasses and bodies of water using colors and symbols.

- A transportation map show how you can travel from one place to another. Some transportation maps show major and minor roads. Others show bus, train, and boat routes.

- A historical map shows information about past events and places. These maps often show place names and political boundaries that differ from those today.

TEACH

- Ask students to turn to **Student WorkText, page 94.**

- Have students read the page silently before discussing together the sample map and steps to read it.

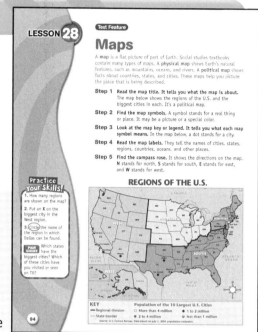

TEACHER THINK ALOUD This map is a political map. First, I look at the title. It tells me that the map shows the United States divided into its major regions, or areas.

Next I look at the labels. The name of each region is written in capital letters. In addition, the abbreviation for each state name is given as well as the names and locations of several large cities. For example, I see the location of Chicago in the Midwest region.

Now, I look at the key to see what the different circles mean. I see that each circle relates to the number of people living in each city. Finally, I look carefully at the map and think about what information it provides.

- Have students follow the directions and answer the questions under *Practice Your Skills*. Check their answers and assist them, as needed, in interpreting the map.

PRACTICE

- Ask students to turn to **Student WorkText, page 95.** Have them preview the article and complete the *Before You Read* prompt. (See **Preview Routine, page 20**.)

- Ask students to read the article silently, paying special attention to the map. Tell them to answer the *As You Read* questions on their own.

STUDENT THINK ALOUD Have students model aloud how they read the map. Encourage students to share alternate approaches. Use the following prompts as needed:

✔ What did you look at first?

✔ How did you know what country you are looking at?

✔ How did you figure out which state has the most Native American tribes?

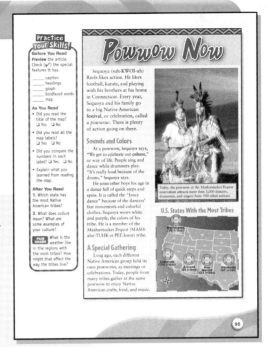

- Discuss the article and map using the *After You Read* questions. You may also wish to ask: *Which state has more Native American tribes—Arizona or Oklahoma? In which region do most of these tribes live?* Have volunteers share their pair-share discussion with the class.

Retelling Model retelling the text. If needed, demonstrate "look backs" by rereading aloud particular parts of the article to refresh students' memories.

APPLY

- Ask students to turn to **Student WorkText, page 96.**

- Have students use The Facts list to create a map. Assist them, as needed.

- Use the *You Be the Expert!* question to spark discussion about the map and help students interpret the information it contains.

- You may wish to continue the discussion with these and other questions:

✔ How many American Indians live in North Dakota?

✔ Which states have more than 100,000 American Indians?

✔ Which state has fewer American Indians—Hawaii or Iowa?

✔ How is information in list form different from information in a map? Which is easier for you to read? **NAEP**

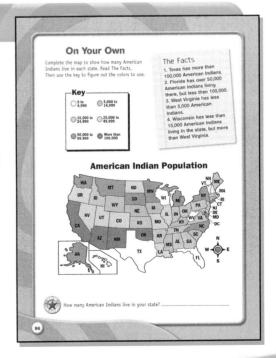

LESSON 29 Maps

CONNECTING TO YOUR CURRICULUM

Maps

You will find these and other maps in your social studies and science textbooks. Use these as opportunities to reinforce students' skills.

Social Studies

- physical maps of regions in the United States
- state product maps
- landform maps of the United States
- political maps of North America (United States, Canada, Mexico)
- historical maps, such as one of the 13 Colonies
- bodies-of-water maps

Science

- weather maps
- climate maps
- world ecosystems map
- rain forest maps

TEACH

- Ask students to turn to **Student WorkText, page 97**.

- Have students read the page silently before discussing together the sample map and steps to read it.

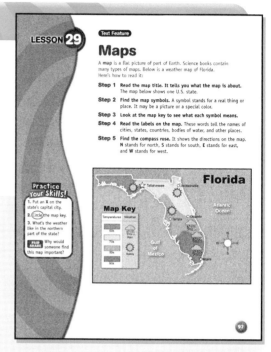

TEACHER THINK ALOUD First I'll read the title to find out what the map is about. This map shows the weather in Florida. Next, I'll read each label. The labels name the state, cities, and bodies of water that are important. I'll also remember to read the map key to see what information it adds. As I read, I will think about how the information in the map goes together.

- Have students follow the directions and answer the questions under *Practice Your Skills*. Check their answers and assist them, as needed, in interpreting the map.

PRACTICE

- Ask students to turn to **Student WorkText, page 98.** Have them preview the article and complete the *Before You Read* prompt.

- Ask students to read the article silently, paying special attention to the map. Tell them to answer the *As You Read* questions on their own.

STUDENT THINK ALOUD Have students model aloud how they read the map. Use the following prompts as needed:

- ✔ Which labels are most important on the map?
- ✔ What does the map key tell you?
- ✔ How does the map relate to the article?
- ✔ How do the other text features relate to the article?

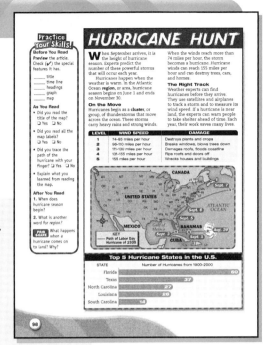

- Discuss the article and map using the *After You Read* questions. You may also wish to ask: *How long was the hurricane on land?*

- Have volunteers share their pair-share discussion with the class.

Retelling Model retelling the text. Involve students by having them add one or two of the details. If needed, demonstrate "look backs" by rereading aloud particular parts of the article to refresh student's memories.

APPLY

- Ask students to turn to **Student WorkText, page 99.**

- Have students study the map in order to add information and write questions about its content.

- Ask students to trade papers with a partner and answer each other's questions. Then provide time for all students to share their questions and answers with the whole class.

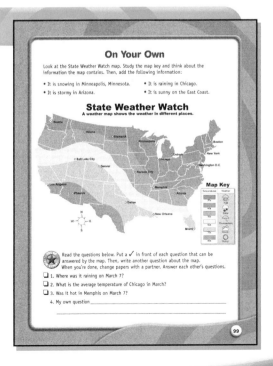

TEACH

Text Structure: Description

- Discuss the importance of identifying how a text is structured. Tell students that figuring out how a selection is structured will help them organize their thinking as they read. Explain that a writer often uses signal words as clues to what the text structure is. Display the **Text Structures Poster.** (See **Student WorkText, page 105.**)

> **TEACHER THINK ALOUD** I know that writers organize their writing in a way that helps us better understand and remember the information. In the article "One Language, Many Nations" the writer tells about different places around the world in which Spanish is spoken. As I read, I will look for the name of each nation and special details about it. I'll look for clue words that help me.

Build Background: Smart Chart

- Use the **Smart Chart Routine, page 19.** Through your questioning, guide the discussion to identify students' knowledge and/or misconceptions about immigration or where Spanish is spoken around the world.

Preteach Vocabulary

- Define each of the following words from "One Language, Many Nations." Provide a context sentence and point out any related words or important word parts. (See **Vocabulary Routine, page 21.**)

traditions   A custom, idea, or belief that is handed down from one generation to the next. *Thanksgiving is a tradition my family celebrates every year.*
Related word: *traditional*

ancient   Very old; belonging to a time long ago. *An ancient tomb of a pharaoh was found in Egypt.*
Related word: *old*

population The total number of people who live in a place.
The population of my town is now more than 5,000.
Common word part: *-tion*
Related words: *populate, populated, popular*

citizen A member of a particular country who has a right to live there.
I am a citizen of the United States.
Related word: *citizenship*

- Ask students to turn to **Student WorkText, pages 100–101.** Direct their attention to *Before You Read* and have them complete the Related Word Pairs activity before they begin to read the article.

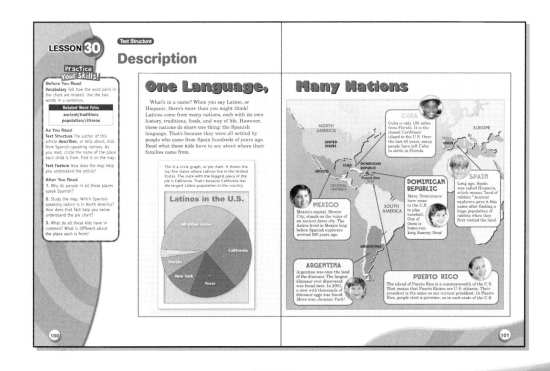

Read the Article

- Read aloud the *As You Read* text to help students set a purpose for reading. Then, ask students to read the article silently, paying special attention to the map.

- When students have finished reading, discuss the article and map using the *After You Read* questions.

Check Comprehension

- Have students retell the selection in their own words. Encourage them to include as many details from the article as they can recall. (See pages 21–23 for a detailed discussion of retellings.)

- You may wish to continue the discussion with these and other questions:

  ✔ In which nation did the Aztecs live?

  ✔ Which nation's name means "land of rabbits"?

  ✔ In which nation are its people also U.S. citizens?

Graphic Organizer

- Ask students to turn to **Student WorkText, page 102**.

- Have them reread the article to determine any information left out of their retellings. Then ask students to complete the graphic organizer to highlight details about each nation.

- When finished, have students do a second retelling to a partner.

- Use a graphic organizer such as this whenever students encounter description paragraphs in their social studies and science textbooks.

Description

Reread "One Language, Many Nations." Fill in the graphic organizer with details about each kid.

We Are Latinos!

Kid's Name	Language Kid Speaks	Where Kid Is From	Interesting Fact About the Nation
Alina	Spanish	Cuba	will vary
Thomas	Spanish	Mexico	will vary
Robert	Spanish	Argentina	will vary
Amanda	Spanish	Dominican Republic	will vary
Carlos	Spanish	Spain	will vary
Paula	Spanish	Puerto Rico	will vary

Retell Use the organizer above to retell "One Language, Many Nations" in your own words. Remember to include details about each kid and the place he or she is from.

102

APPLY

Writing Frame

- Ask students to turn to **Student WorkText, page 103**.

- Have students complete the description writing frame using the information in the article on pages 100–101. Work with students, as needed.

On Your Own

- Have students write their own description paragraph using information from their social studies textbook. Students will describe the countries and languages spoken by classmates' ancestors.

- Explain to students that the more practice they have using the description writing frame, the more familiar they will be with this text structure. This will assist them in recognizing the description pattern as they read, inform them about how to organize their thinking about their reading and writing, and improve their reading comprehension overall.

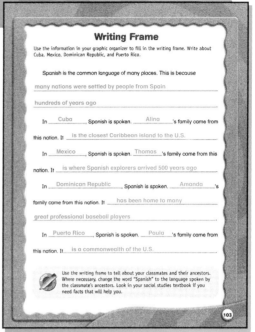

Writing Frame

Use the information in your graphic organizer to fill in the writing frame. Write about Cuba, Mexico, Dominican Republic, and Puerto Rico.

Spanish is the common language of many places. This is because
many nations were settled by people from Spain
hundreds of years ago

In ___Cuba___, Spanish is spoken. ___Alina___'s family came from this nation. It __is the closest Caribbean island to the U.S.__

In ___Mexico___, Spanish is spoken. ___Thomas___'s family came from this nation. It __is where Spanish explorers arrived 500 years ago__

In ___Dominican Republic___, Spanish is spoken. ___Amanda___'s family came from this nation. It __has been home to many great professional baseball players__

In ___Puerto Rico___, Spanish is spoken. ___Paula___'s family came from this nation. It __is a commonwealth of the U.S.__

Use the writing frame to tell about your classmates and their ancestors. Where necessary, change the word "Spanish" to the language spoken by the classmate's ancestors. Look in your social studies textbook if you need facts that will help you.

103

LET'S NAVIGATE

Follow the five easy steps when you read nonfiction text.

5 EASY STEPS

Step ① Preview
Read the title, introduction, and headings. Think about what they tell you.

Step ② Prepare
Say to yourself, "This article is going to be about _____. What do I already know?"

Step ③ Read
Carefully read the article.

Step ④ Use the Tools
Stop at special features, such as the special type and the graphics. Ask yourself,

- Why is this here?
- What does it tell me?
- How does it connect to the article?

Step ⑤ Retell/Connect
Retell what you learned. Think about how it connects to your life and the world.

① # THE AMAZING OCTOPUS

The octopus is an awesome ocean animal. It can be as HUGE as 30 feet or as tiny as 1 inch in length. What makes this creature so amazing?

Body Parts

③ An octopus has 8 arms that it uses to swim and to catch food. An octopus has suction cups on the back of its arms.

④ **Suction cups** help the octopus grab a meal, such as crabs, clams, and fish. If an octopus loses an arm, it can grow another one. This is called **regeneration** (ree-gen-uh-RAY-shun). A starfish can do the same thing.

An octopus has no bones, so its body is soft and squishy. This allows it to squeeze into small spaces. An octopus can squeeze into a seashell! This helps the octopus chase food even into little cracks.

Survival Skills ②

Octopuses have many ways to avoid their enemies. An octopus can change colors as **camouflage** (KAM-uh-flahzh), a way to blend in with its surroundings. That way, its enemies can't see it. And, in the blink of an eye, it can make its skin bumpy. To an enemy, the octopus looks like just another rock!

An octopus can also squirt purple-black ink at its enemies. The enemy can't see the octopus through the ink, and the octopus can quickly swim away to safety.

⑤

Sequence

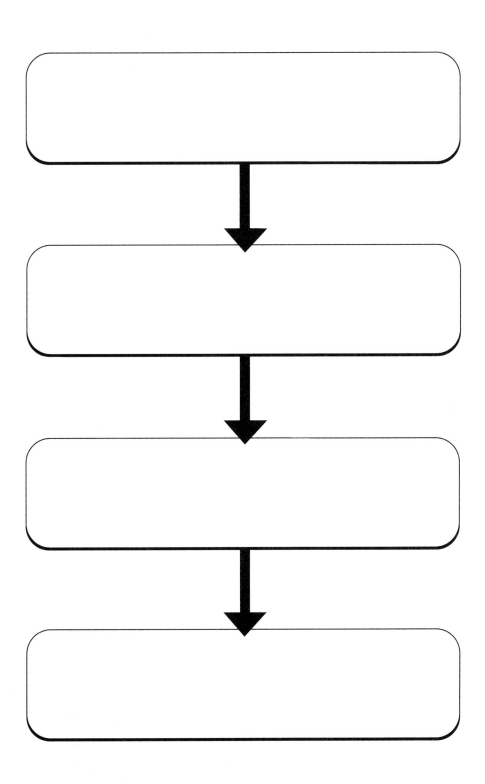

Compare/Contrast

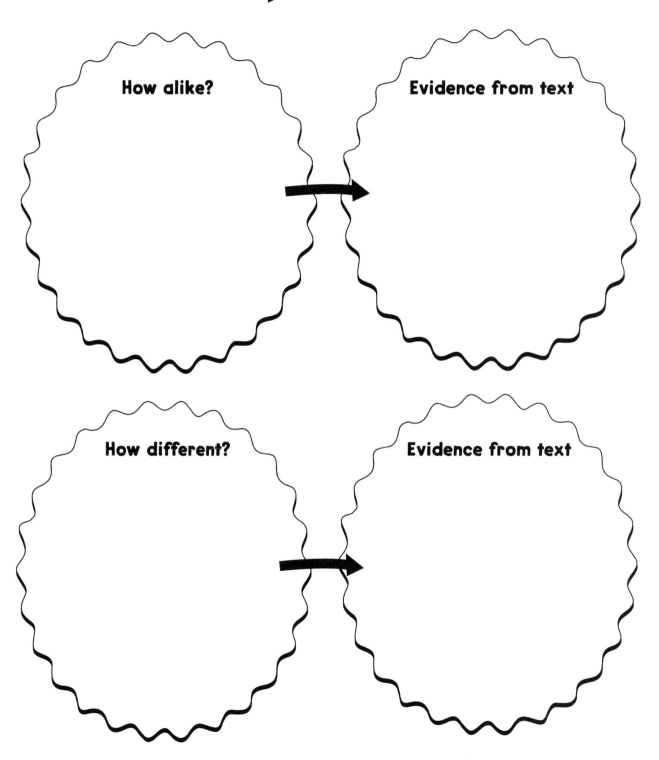

How alike?

Evidence from text

How different?

Evidence from text

Cause/Effect

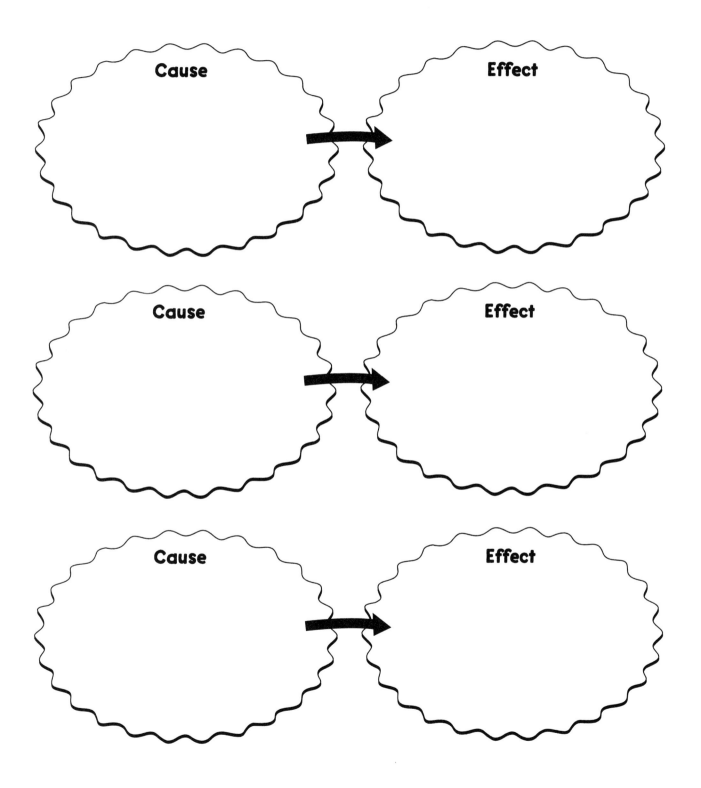

Cause

Effect

Cause

Effect

Cause

Effect

Problem/Solution

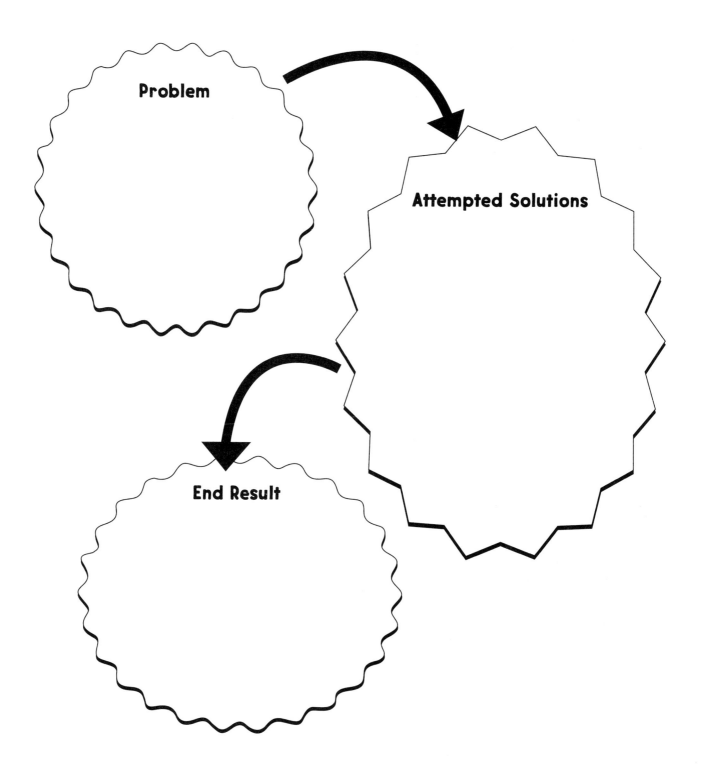

Problem

Attempted Solutions

End Result

Description

Main Idea _____

_____

Detail 1 _____

_____

Detail 2 _____

_____

Detail 3 _____

_____

Detail 4 _____

_____

Bibliography

Alvermann, D.E., & Phelps, S.F. (1998). *Content reading and literacy: Succeeding in today's diverse classrooms.* (2nd ed.). Needham Heights, MA: Allyn & Bacon.

Carnine, D.W., Silbert, J., & Kameenui, E.J. (1997). *Direct instruction reading.* (3rd ed.). Upper Saddle River, NJ: Prentice-Hall.

Chall, J.S. (1983). *Stages of reading development.* New York: McGraw-Hill.

Cooper, J.D. (1993). *Literacy: Helping children construct meaning.* (2nd ed.). Boston: Houghton Mifflin Company.

CORE (Consortium on Reading Excellence). (1999). Novato, CA: Arena Press.

Duke, N.K., & Bennett-Armisted, V.S. (2003). *Reading and writing informational text in the primary grades.* New York: Scholastic Inc.

Graves, M., Juel, C., & Graves, B. (1998). *Teaching reading in the 21st Century.* Needham Heights, MA: Allyn & Bacon.

Lapp, D., Flood, J., & Farnan, N. (1996). *Content area reading and learning: Instructional strategies.* (2nd ed.). Needham Heights, MA: Allyn & Bacon.

Moss, B. (2003). *Exploring the literature of fact.* New York: The Guilford Press.

Moss, B. (2004). Teaching expository text structures through informational trade book retellings. *The Reading Teacher*, 57(8), 710–718.

Vacca, R.T., & Vacca, J.L. (1999). *Content area reading: Literacy and learning across the curriculum.* (6th ed.). New York: Addison-Wesley Educational Publishers Inc.